Kitchens

DESIGNS FOR LIVING

Kitchens

DESIGNS FOR LIVING

Angela Phelan

MetroBooks

MetroBooks

An Imprint of Friedman/Fairfax Publishers

Library of Congress Cataloging-in-Publication Data

Phelan, Angela.
    Kitchens / by Angela Phelan
        p.   cm.
    Includes index.
    ISBN 1-56799-295-1 (hardcover)
    1. Kitchens. 2. Interior decoration. I. Title.
NK2117.K5P48   1996
747.7'97—dc20   95-48069
                                 CIP

Editor: Susan Lauzau
Art Director: Jeff Batzli
Designer: Andrea Karman
Photography Editor: Samantha Larrance
Production Associate: Camille Lee

Color separations by Bright Arts (Singapore) Pte. Ltd.
Printed in China by Leefung-Asco Printers Ltd.

For bulk purchases and special sales, please contact:
Friedman / Fairfax Publishers
Attention: Sales Department
15 West 26th Street
New York, NY 10010
212/685-6610 FAX 212/685-1307

Dedicated to the memory of Nonna Ruggeri,

in whose kitchen glorious food and gentle instruction

inspired four generations of mothers and daughters.

C o n t e n t s

❈❈❈

❈❈❈

❈❈❈

❈❈❈

Kitchens for the Way We Live

In a majority of households, the kitchen could more accurately be termed the living room. It is in the kitchen that meals are prepared and, often, eaten; homework and school projects are completed, away from the "good" furniture in the parlor or dining room; pets are fed; laundry is folded; and family matters are discussed around the reassuring warmth of the kitchen table.

But this has not always been so. Over the centuries, the character of the kitchen has changed, reflecting with each metamorphosis the evolving culture it served. In medieval times, the kitchens of castles and abbeys were vast affairs that included bakeries and breweries and led to nearby vegetable gardens, slaughtering pens, fishponds, and dovecotes, all contributing to the mammoth task of feeding the scores (and in some cases hundreds) of people who lived and worked within the castle walls. The mistress was intimately involved in the running of the household, though cooks were most often male, as great strength was required to maneuver the large cauldrons and withstand the smoke and heat of primitive chimneys.

In colonial America, too, the kitchen was the hub of family life, as the house usually consisted of only one large room—the keeping room—though if the family was fairly well off there may have been separate sleeping chambers. Food was prepared and preserved, cloth was spun, and babies were rocked while the blazing fire kept the entire room warm. But as a prosperous middle class emerged and the Industrial Revolution rolled through Europe and the United States, life in the kitchen changed on both continents. In

ABOVE: Your kitchen can get a facelift even if you don't plan to make expensive changes such as replacing cabinets and other fixtures. These careworn cupboards have been stripped of old paint and then washed with a golden color, creating a sunny climate no matter the weather. Diamonds, both vertical and horizontal, in a deeper hue of the same color family punctuate cabinet panels, drawer faces, and even the dishwasher. New hardware can change the look of cabinets even without changes to the paint finish: here, porcelain knobs and brass drawer pulls add old-fashioned charm. Terra-cotta pots filled with forced bulbs pick up the yellow-orange of the diamonds and take a few steps further down the color spectrum toward red; cream and loden striped curtains vary the geometric theme, mirroring the slender vertical stems of blooming amaryllis and paper whites.

OPPOSITE: Today's kitchens often function as impromptu family conference centers, as well as places to cook and serve meals. This sunlit space adjusts well to its variable status, flowing comfortably from kitchen to informal dining area to open living room. A marble counter with dropped-in cooktop is stove, work surface, and room divider in one; the chunky fixture defines the kitchen area without divorcing it from the space as a whole. Glass-front pine cabinets contribute to the airy feeling and echo the lines of undressed French doors. Built-in cushioned benches in a practical L-shape, together with two pull-up chairs, provide plenty of seating for guests to relax and chat with the cook or for children to complete homework as busy parents prepare for dinner. But as fabulously functional as this kitchen is, it is the warmth of personal touches that makes the room truly special: an array of Mexican folk art and textiles infuses the kitchen with the spirit of a collection carefully and happily gathered.

Victorian times, a lady was seldom seen in the kitchen, which was run by a staff of servants. Her domain was the parlor, dining room, and sitting room, from whence she issued orders to her domestics on the tasks to be carried out in the kitchen.

This state continued until World War I, when jobs for women in factories became available. As good domestic help grew scarce, the lady of the house was obliged to take up kitchen duty herself. With more and more women working in their own kitchens, manufacturers recognized an opportunity to market new and improved gadgets and time-saving appliances.

But this renewed interest in the kitchen was not to last: by the sixties, middle-class women were plunging into the workforce, and as with each cultural change, the kitchen changed too. The seventies and eighties saw the advent of the "convenience" kitchen, where the object was to get in and out as quickly as possible. Food was defrosted, heated, and served on paper plates, which were casually tossed in the trash—then the family rushed off to do more important things.

In the nineties, we've come to understand that our families and our own well-being *are* the important things. We've revived our kitchens in the colonial sense—they've again become the heart of the home. But this is not to say that all kitchens serve the same functions. Some of us are single and use our kitchens to prepare romantic dinners or as buffet space at parties; others of us are at the centers of rambling families that look forward to traditional Sunday suppers and cookie baking at holiday time.

Before you begin to plan your kitchen, consider how you will live in it. Are you a serious cook who can't bear to be without professional equipment? Do you prefer to prepare uncomplicated meals but delight in the table settings? Is it your habit to leave belongings scattered about, or are you a minimalist in philosophy as well as taste? Your answers, together with the hundreds of ideas you'll find in the pages of this book, will help you plan the best kitchen for your lifestyle.

The amount of space devoted to the kitchen, existing features and fittings, and the amount of money you plan to spend will also affect the decisions you make. Here you'll find a range of solutions that suit your style, whether you have a tiny galley kitchen or a spacious great room. No matter what the size of your pocketbook or the state of your existing kitchen, page after page of glorious color photographs invite you to contemplate various layouts, unusual furniture choices, and bold new color schemes. An array of kitchens in various sizes and styles define the ultimate in efficiency without sacrificing beauty. Explore, too, the extras that can make your kitchen so valuable as the center of your home: you'll find potted herb and vegetable gardens, built-in office space, integral play spaces, laundry areas, and much more. Finally, the ingredients of a successful kitchen are laid out one by one, showing options for sinks, stoves, refrigerators, surfaces, and lighting.

The modern kitchen is cooking area, pantry, and dining room; it is also playroom, study, and family room. Once again, we've adapted the concept of "kitchen" to suit our lifestyles, resulting in a space that is beautiful, functional, and easy to live in.

ABOVE: This airy kitchen is by definition part of the living space, since no walls separate it from other areas. Instead, pine planks ground the entire great room, linking kitchen and living room in a wash of honey-blond wood. The unadorned windows of the clerestory admit streams of natural light and add a quiet grace to this unpretentious room.

ABOVE: Elements both stately and whimsical mix comfortably in this unabashedly eccentric kitchen. Swathes of gold fabric frame potted standards that fill a wide picture window in an impressive display of Classical symmetry. Cabinets in antique white, a stone floor, and hardware of twisted iron likewise contribute to the air of old-world formality, but this aura of elegance is broken by seat covers in a wild zebra print, a bold-check rug, and dishtowels emblazoned with sheep. Don't be afraid to let your imagination take over when planning your ideal kitchen. While design "rules" abound, remember that fabulous new trends are often the result of wayward decorators' refusal to obey the dictates of current fashion. A playful spirit and a sense of adventure can be key in designing a kitchen that suits you and your family.

Chapter One

Kitchens That Deliver

Planning a good kitchen—one that you and your family will feel happy and comfortable in—is part of the joy of renovating or redecorating. There are several steps to creating the kitchen that will deliver for you.

First, make several lists. List number one should enumerate all the tasks and activities that you perform in your kitchen and should include those activities you would like to move into the kitchen. A sample list might read: prepare meals; supervise children's homework; write letters; pay bills; store wine collection and professional cookware; display heirloom china. Your second list should consist of the cooking and kitchen equipment you already own and those pieces you would like to add, including special cabinets, chairs, and so on.

Next, make a simple drawing of the space you're dealing with, keeping in mind the peripheral areas—such as a back porch or terrace,

foyer, dining room, or pantry—that can be annexed to the main space. Draw the room to scale, using graph paper and working in pencil so that you can correct any mistakes. Also make overhead-view drawings of movable pieces, such as tables and chairs, that you plan to put into your kitchen, and cut these items out. Draw as movable objects any usually stationary pieces that you are willing to pull out and place elsewhere, like the oven or sink. You will first have to measure all walls, cabinets, appliances, furniture, and anything else that must fit into the kitchen.

The third step in planning your kitchen involves laying out the physical space. Using your room plan and the movable pieces you've cut out, lay out the kitchen you would like to have. Be audacious! Only you know, after years of living with kitchens that fell far short of your needs, how this space can be arranged to fulfill your dreams.

ABOVE: A good kitchen provides lots of light, counter space, and storage, along with a pleasant atmosphere and details that reflect your personal style. This homey kitchen offers a view of the garden through simple tieback curtains. There's plenty of counter space to display the cook's flowers as well as for the more mundane tasks like chopping vegetables. Painted baskets that coordinate with the blooms echo the pattern of the wallpaper. These soft pastels are picked up again in the dishtowels and mugs—subtle and inexpensive touches that make for a pulled-together look.

✖ ✖ ✖

OPPOSITE: The kitchen that looks good to you is the kitchen that works for you. Cherry cabinets, hanging baskets, and mullioned windows convey a sense of warmth and tradition in this relaxed family space. Within easy distance of kitchen work surfaces yet far enough away to keep onlookers from getting underfoot, the country dining table is perfect for homework, casual lunches, and craft projects with the little ones.

As you plan, be aware of certain limitations. For instance, if you would like a gas range and the nearest gas line is miles away, your wish may be impractical. If this is the case, research propane stoves or consider some of the new electric ranges as alternatives. Since water lines are expensive to run, try to organize your plan so that water needs (the sink, the dishwasher, laundry facilities) are grouped together near any existing water lines.

The source lists at the back of this book, as well as your local telephone directory, will be invaluable in conducting your research. You'll need to call your utility companies—gas, electric, water—if you are going to make radical changes. You'll also want to look into various options for your cooking equipment. Do you want a restaurant range or will one of the newer lines of professional ranges designed for residences suffice? Visit the showrooms of major suppliers of kitchen equipment and explore the offerings. Ask lots of questions and measure everything you think you might like. Keep with you a little notebook of measurements of your dream kitchen (include ceiling height, doorway widths, and dimensions of any immovable objects) so that you'll have some idea of whether the new pieces are in the realm of possibility.

If you are installing or replacing cabinetry, you now have all the measurements you need to begin searching for the ideal cupboards. But remember that yards of linear cabinets are often a joy only to the company that sells them. Visit as many displays in home remodeling shops as you can; the photographs in this book will also help you decide which style is best suited to your needs. Investigate cabinet refacing as well. The purchase of cabinetry can be the most costly part of kitchen remodeling, so it is wise to look carefully at what exists. You may be able to get the cabinets you want by simply painting them and replacing hardware.

When doing extensive remodeling, you will most likely need to hire a contractor. This step can be fraught with pitfalls, and the hassles of working with contractors are legendary. Often, problems are the result of poor choices based on emotion or on the skill of the salesperson. The first and most important thing to remember at this phase is your budget. Secure three bids from reputable dealers. A personal referral from a friend is a good way to find a reliable contractor and allows you to see their work firsthand, but if you haven't turned up any good candidates this way, ask your local Better Business Bureau for a list of suppliers. Resist the nearly overwhelming temptation to rush through this stage. Get the bids, evaluate each one, and make your choice after a personal interview with each candidate.

With these simple steps carefully researched, you are well on your way to the kitchen that will deliver exactly what you want.

❊❊❊

ABOVE: Well-planned kitchens make effective use of all available space. This table recesses into the existing cabinetry and looks like a drawer when pushed back. Great for solo meals, it also serves as an extra surface for setting materials during complicated cooking projects. A mirror behind the counter extends the space visually, and glass cabinets with recessed lighting display jewel-toned dishes and glassware. This attractive and efficient setup is ideal for small apartments and studios, where the kitchen is likely to be in full view of living areas.

✶✶✶

ABOVE: Kitchens with modest dimensions are often the most efficient—all appliances, cookware, work surfaces, and supplies are within a few steps of one another, preventing much needless to and fro. This wraparound tile counter defines the kitchen area, but the open design prevents the small space from feeling claustrophobic. Plenty of storage in undercounter cabinets allows most kitchen equipment to be stashed out of sight, which is particularly important when the cooking area is constantly on display. By stocking the cupboard in the living/dining area with forties-style dishware and leaving select pieces resting atop the kitchen counter, the two rooms are given continuity; the solution is also a practical one, since a dining room full of dishes means extra space in the kitchen for pots, pans, utensils, and groceries.

ISLANDS

*T*oday an island is almost a requisite, whether the kitchen is cozy country style or sleekly modern. Descendants of the old-fashioned worktable, these paragons of kitchen virtue now house everything from microwave ovens to vegetable sinks. Custom-built islands allow you to indulge all your dreams, but stock units with a variety of options and in a range of styles are available at a fraction of the cost.

▣ Choose an island that is in proportion to your kitchen space. If you have a vast, unused area in the center of your kitchen, go ahead and select an expansive unit, but if your space is limited, scale back accordingly. Ideally, an island should not interfere with efficient movement between the three most important pieces in your kitchen: sink, stove, and refrigerator.

▣ Islands may be topped with any number of surfaces: marble is ideal for working with dough because its surface remains smooth and cool, while hardwood or butcher block is ideal for chopping vegetables and other preparatory tasks. Excellent heat resistance makes tile a good choice if the island will be situated near the oven or stove, since the surface can serve as a rest for hot pans. A wooden top with a tile inset offers the best of both these worlds. Synthetic surfaces can be attractive, durable, and easy to clean, but study your material of choice well before you buy: some are easily nicked and scarred by knives and can be permanently stained by various chemicals.

▣ Think about the added fixtures that are most important to you. A microwave built into the island frees up counter or cabinet space elsewhere, while a sink close to a work surface is particularly handy for rinsing vegetables and cleaning up utensils and cutting boards. Range tops dropped right into the island are another popular option—the additional space around the cooking area allows for maximum efficiency and comfort. Some islands may also be fitted with a mini refrigerator, cooled vegetable bins, or a warming drawer. Nearly all units are equipped with extra electrical outlets, which are necessary to power the various food processors, mixers, and blenders that have become essential to the modern cook. Note that all these bonus items require electrical wiring, water pipes, or gas lines that your kitchen may not yet be set up for; it's important to factor in these preparations when calculating the overall cost of your island.

▣ Storage is another asset that makes an island worth considering. Taking stock of the items in your kitchen will help you decide how best to utilize the storage space you'll gain. If you have lots of table linens and tiny gadgets, drawers of various sizes are probably your best bet. Cabinets will store pots and serving pieces, while a divided rack can stash cookie sheets and cutting boards. Bins for collecting recyclables are another increasingly popular addition.

▣ Also consider how your island will be used. Will it chiefly be a work space or do you plan to eat informal meals there? In either case, a counter overhang or a recessed space beneath the top, which allows a chair to be pulled up comfortably, is highly desirable. Since so many kitchen tasks must be performed while standing, frenetic cooks will appreciate the opportunity to sit as they chop vegetables or keep an eye on the soufflé. If you'd like to serve breakfasts and snacks at your island, a bilevel model—which includes a surface at work height and a lower counter at dining height—may be a practical option.

ABOVE: Islands can be as decorative as they are practical. This attractive, marble-topped unit, with its integrated glass-front cabinet, adds as much to the room's beauty as it does to the efficiency of the kitchen.

ABOVE: Wipe-clean tile in hunter green, highlighted by sleek white cabinetry, extends all the way to the ceiling in this modest kitchen. A tile wall treatment is effective in rooms where only one or two walls need to be covered—four tiled walls may look sterile and can produce unpleasant acoustics. The cooking peninsula maximizes space and separates the kitchen from an adjoining sitting area while offering seating for informal meals. An oriental rug bedecked with fruits and flowers sets off a colorful collection of majolica.

❋ ❋ ❋

ABOVE: This traditional black-and-white kitchen features an enormous island with maple chopping-block surfaces. Accents of red spark up countertops and line the shelves of glass-front white cabinets. Open soffits provide additional storage and create a wonderful, out-of-the-way display space for vintage commercial signs or other collectibles. Leaving the area beneath the ceiling open makes the room airier and gives you the option of stenciling a decorative border around the entire perimeter of the room.

❊❊❊

ABOVE: Arts and Crafts–style cabinetry combines with natural materials in granite countertops, birch flooring, and an oak ceiling to infuse this simple space with a sense of calm. The subtle palette of muted greens and wood tones from pale to earthy contribute to the contemplative aura; large picture windows and a cutout above the counter keep air and light streaming into this serene kitchen.

ABOVE LEFT: To maximize efficiency, a wall of this kitchen's eating area has been converted into a work space by the addition of elegant, side-by-side glass-front cabinets and a counter complete with sink. The white-on-white effect of milky plates and clear glass against the pristine surfaces of the cabinetry is truly breathtaking, and thanks to the proximity of the table, dishware and linens travel quickly from strorage to dinner.

❈ ❈ ❈

ABOVE RIGHT: Painted panels on cabinets here extend to the face of a sub-zero refrigerator in an inspiring show of unity. The butcher-block unit—which does double duty as a chopping surface and extra storage space—affixes to the counter with tiny brass hooks, but can be unhinged to roll to a sink, range top, or wherever else it's needed. Note that the permanent counter also houses a cabinet; its door ingeniously opens on its right side rather than its front.

❈ ❈ ❈

OPPOSITE: The cool, clean efficiency of this well-designed kitchen is enhanced by a floating island. This attractive task center rolls easily on metal casters, bringing ample counter space right to the range, the sink, or anywhere in between. Then it slides to the dishwasher for quick cleanup of cookware. And the piece is so handsome that it may be loaded with goodies and rolled into the dining room to take on the role of a sideboard.

✻✻✻

ABOVE: A small table tucked into a cozy corner is handy to essential comforts—a telephone and hot coffee. Open shelves near the table collect cookbooks, making planning for meals and parties a snap. The ticking-striped bench cover lifts to reveal a deep chest for storing table linens. With the addition of favorite art and bundles of dried flowers and herbs, even inexpensive pieces of furniture like this melamine-topped table and pair of wooden stools create a homey kitchen nook.

ABOVE: This large work island offers surface burners, a deep sink, and a perch for breakfast. Note the refrigerator recessed into the back wall; its bead-board panels and old-fashioned hardware are in perfect keeping with the country feel of the room. The lineup of white cookie jars along the spice shelf imparts a whimsical touch to a space that might otherwise seem somewhat austere.

ABOVE LEFT: Whitewashed open shelves flanking the walls offer ample storage as well a feast for the eye. But selection and placement of these items is not as random as it looks. Grouping objects from the same color families but in a variety of hues—such as pieces in shades of cobalt, pale blue, cream, and white—allows a look that is unified yet has pleasing contrasts.

✾ ✾ ✾

ABOVE RIGHT: This room announces the return of the kitchen table. Set in great light, this sturdy-legged table, paired with a set of stained chairs, lends itself to all manner of chores, informal meetings, and, of course, meals. The exchange of storage space and efficiency for comfort is definitely worth considering. The casual look of the table is carried throughout the kitchen—wooden plank floors painted battleship gray, open shelving with dozens of nooks and crannies, metal-screened utility lighting, and a Dutch door all contribute to the porchlike ambience.

✾ ✾ ✾

OPPOSITE: A feeling of warmth, brought on by the lambent light and the unstudied mix of items, suffuses this space. A collection of china is lit within mullioned, glass-front cabinets. Rectangular tiles laid like bricks serve as a backsplash, while square tiles set on point provide contrasting pattern on the countertop. A restaurant stove and hood, trimmed with brass, invite the cook to linger, while potted plants, a pitcherful of wooden utensils, and antique canisters add to the casual charm.

ABOVE LEFT: Even a small apartment can usually find room for a lineup of appliances and fixtures that will serve admirably as a kitchen. In this studio space, only one wall is devoted to the "kitchen"; a trestle table has been set up to further define the kitchen area and to function as an additional work surface in a setup that has limited counter space. The Provençal pattern of the wallpaper and swag, which is visible from the living area, is sophisticated enough to blend with couches and chairs.

❋ ❋ ❋

ABOVE RIGHT: You needn't sacrifice a comfortable preparation area, even if space is at a premium. This stool, often seen in medical offices, operates quietly and quickly with a hydraulic lift system, and its metal casters allow it to move conveniently out of the way when kitchen tasks are finished. A work surface swings out from the counter so that the cook can sit with knees tucked snugly underneath.

❋ ❋ ❋

OPPOSITE: Space may be tight in this city kitchen, but it functions with supreme efficiency despite the limitations. A built-in microwave oven sits atop a low wall oven, conserving precious counter space. To eliminate the need for cabinet storage of large pots and pans, a rack has been installed down the length of the galley space; if you consider this solution for your own kitchen, measure carefully to be sure that the hanging pots won't interfere with opening cabinet doors. A counter laid below the window provides an extra work surface, complete with stools that offer the cook and accomplices respite as they chop veggies or ice cupcakes. Mirrored backsplashes behind range top and counter do their part to expand space visually, and the undressed window—besides admitting maximum light—underscores the simplicity of the decor. Cabinets with textured, colored glass panels are a brilliant choice here; they show only the silhouettes of contents, avoiding a messy look while escaping the closed-in feeling that solid cabinets would give in this small a space.

ABOVE LEFT: When natural light is absent from your kitchen, consider creating a sunny mood with color. The nonconformity of the lemon yellow ceiling is grounded by the traditional black-and-white tile floor and simple, white appliances and cabinetry. Vibrantly striped wallpaper mixes companionably with the checkerboard border of a framed print. The yellow and chrome tractor-seat stool is both functional and funky.

❊ ❊ ❊

ABOVE RIGHT: Built-in refrigerators, ovens, and cabinets in traditional cherry are punctuated by a beautifully mullioned window. A marble-topped counter beneath the window ties together the right and left sides of the space, which often appear divorced in a galley kitchen. The counter's position allows all four flanking cabinets to open while capitalizing on space that is often lost. As every serious baker knows, cool marble provides an ideal surface for rolling pastry dough; the area below accommodates wicker baskets filled with dry goods.

❊❊❊

ABOVE: It's particularly important to remember personal taste when decorating an area like the kitchen, where so little of the furniture is movable once set in place. The austere simplicity of this modern kitchen, with its angled white cabinets, recessed lighting, and accents in geometrical shapes and primary colors, will quickly lose its charm if you tend to accumulate lots of objects around you, requiring a struggle to maintain the sleek, uncluttered look of this design. On the other hand, those with a yen for the elemental will revel in this kitchen's clean lines, basic colors, and modern forms.

❈ ❈ ❈

ABOVE: Warm wood tones in the form of a stained maple tabletop and four occasional chairs are central to the atmosphere of this room. Curtained cupboards are juxtaposed with a bare window; dressing glass-front cabinets this way is a beautiful solution for hiding cluttered shelves. The large painting over the stove is an unusual addition and offers a touch of formality—if you decide to follow suit, make sure you don't use a treasured piece, since the moisture and oils from cooking are likely to eventually damage the painting. Copper kettle and bowl and a framed print also contribute to the inherent elegance of the room.

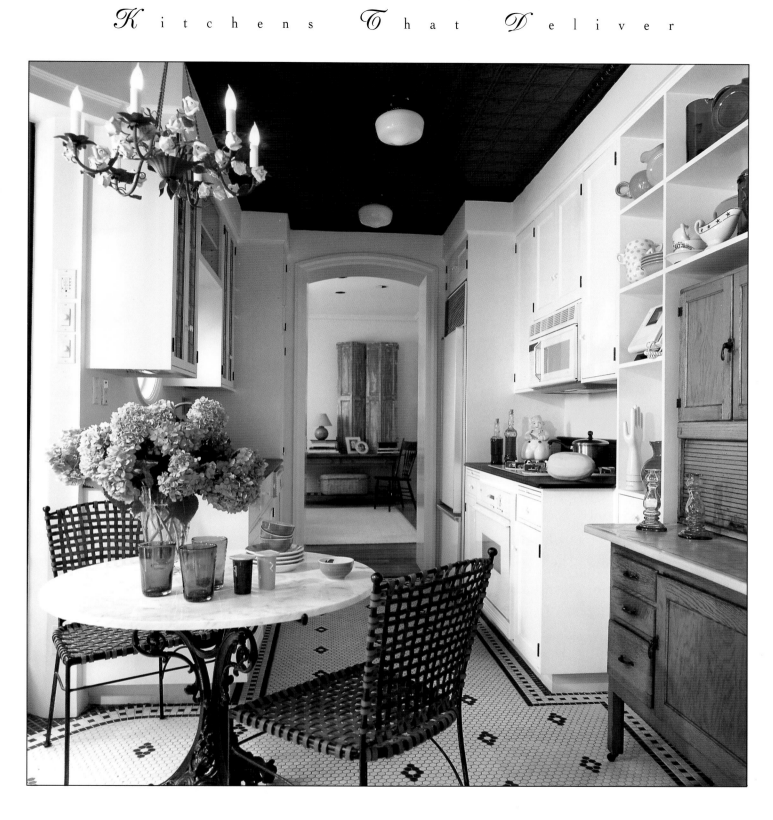

✳✳✳

ABOVE: A bistro table and two chairs tucked into a sunny niche provide a welcome break in a galley kitchen. Note the Hoosier cupboard against the right wall. These wonderful units can still be found in country antique shops. Designed as stand-alone pastry centers, most are fitted with a large-capacity flour sifter behind a tambour door and an enamel counter for kneading bread or rolling pie crusts. Cabinets above and below accomodate bowls, while utility drawers store spoons, rolling pins, and other implements. The charming look of the Hoosier cupboard makes it worth hunting for if it will fit into your space.

Chapter Two

Eye on Design

great architect once said that good design is the ability to put things in the places they belong. Unfortunately, design sense—the ability to put objects, patterns, and colors where they can best be enjoyed—does not come easily to everyone.

When decorating your kitchen, consider color, light, shape, and scale. Often, we study these elements when designing a living room. Or a bedroom. Or almost any other room in the house. The functional nature of the kitchen prompts us to overlook the finer points of decor and excuse the bland, utilitarian character that has so permeated the kitchen design of the past.

Whether your style is minimalist or traditional, you can use color as a stand-out feature. Judicious use of a single color can unify a kitchen, which is usually a mixture of many bulky shapes.

The color can be as bold as Chinese red or as subtle as celery green. But do consider how you will feel when confronted with these choices day after day. Live with your decision in your mind for a few weeks before you actually execute it.

Color on the ceiling—robin's-egg blue, for instance—is an unusual touch that will radiate soft light. This technique is favored for the ceilings of country porches, and is sure to impart a relaxing feel. Floors, cabinets, and furniture can all benefit from a goodly dose of color. Resist buying appliances in decorator colors, however. These expensive pieces of equipment tend to outlive the color schemes that surround them and thus are best avoided. Stick to the simple and timeless—white, ivory, black, or stainless steel.

Pattern is usually injected with the help of fabric (on cushions, curtains, and table linens) and wallpaper, but can also be part of

ABOVE: Just one unusual element can give your kitchen one-of-a-kind appeal. Subtly colored, handmade tiles in shades of amber, butter yellow, periwinkle, and sea green have been incised with spirals, squiggles, and rays reminiscent of Anasazi rock art to create a stunning yet practical backsplash.

❋ ❋ ❋

OPPOSITE: Glass, metal, and mirrors are warmed by heavy doses of wood and small shots of color. Chairs in a modern design pull up to a curved island, providing extra seating without cluttering the simple space. An adjacent eating area, separated by the stairwell bisecting the room, extends the modern feeling of the kitchen proper. The upholstered chairs offer comfy seating as well as a visual pick-me-up; purposefully mismatched fabric in imperial purple and mini checkerboard are a welcome surprise, adding pattern and color to an otherwise neutral room.

your backsplash or floor via tile or inlaid linoleum. The strong graphics of modern art or the flowery vines of Art Nouveau are wildly different in approach, but both are designs that infuse a room with personality and create visual interest.

You will have the best results if you keep the shape and scale of the room in mind. As you decorate, consider how your choices will affect the character of your kitchen. Dark, hulking cabinets and furniture crammed into a tiny space may well seem oppressively claustrophobic; dainty appointments set in a vast room will likely appear sparse and uninviting.

Nothing creates warmth in a room like beloved possessions. If you are a collector—of dolls, baskets, folk art, pottery—bring a few of your favorite things into the room where you spend most of your

waking time at home. Don't be afraid to display cherished objects in your kitchen, but do take a few precautions. Since the kitchen is often the center of hustle and bustle, place your prized collections within view but safely out of range of disaster. This may mean investing in a glass-front cabinet or a Welsh-style dresser, or it may simply involve installing a plate rail around the perimeter of the room. Soffits and wall niches are also excellent retreats where decorative pieces can be enjoyed without fear of annihilation.

In this chapter, you will find many examples of kitchens with good design, which you can adapt for your own use. As you page through the book, note the decorative touches that appeal to you, and soon you'll be well on your way to putting your things in the places they belong.

OPPOSITE LEFT: Achieve a chic, retro look with a sharp palette of black, white, and red. A dinette table with a funky top, minute yellow tiles above the stove, and glass pieces in hues of cobalt, aquamarine, and jade prevent the simple color scheme from appearing monotonous.

OPPOSITE RIGHT: While the kitchen itself is quite traditional, with its selection of glass-front and paneled white cabinets and floral tile, the bold colors of the ceiling and adjoining wall make a dramatic statement. The deep teal of the ceiling has been painted with a matte finish, while the mulberry of the walls has been ragged for a textured effect. A barnyard motif—carried out in wooden cutouts and a porcelain figure—is a witty reply to the antiseptic quality of pristine white surfaces.

ABOVE: Powerful doses of a single color are the prescription for excitement in this otherwise traditional room. Many people shy away from such vast expanses of strong color, fearing that the effect will be overwhelming, but careful planning can prevent the horrors of excess. Here, a crisp white staircase, mantel, door, and tiles set off the deep cobalt color, and furniture and accessories in warm wood tones help to anchor the room. Attention to decorative details—like the blue-and-white coffeepot, awning-striped pillow, and porcelain drawer and cabinet knobs—gives the space its genteel character. The tiled fireplace, comfy armchair, and sedate grandfather clock bring desired elements of the parlor into this much-lived-in room.

ABOVE: A folk-art mural enhances the Federal style of this charmingly old-fashioned kitchen and dining area. Stylized figures dressed in eighteenth-century garb bring the past into the present day. A series of tiny landscapes and town scenes line the wall below the main mural; a large basket of roses adorns the area above the entryway. If freehand painting is beyond your talents, consider hiring a local artist to carry out your ideas.

❋ ❋ ❋

OPPOSITE: Ragged walls and cabinets give this unusual kitchen the feel of a European country house, complete with aging and uneven plaster. Sprigs of greenery and a cherubic boy adorn the panels of the door and cabinets. Note that a subtle use of trompe l'oeil has created moldings for the drawers and doors; in actuality, all the surfaces are flat.

ABOVE: For a powerful impact, show creativity in your selection of decorative objects and display space. Here, niches of different sizes and shapes have been set into a stark white wall to provide homes for a collection of Mexican dolls. When a collection is composed of pieces with many varied colors and textures, it's best to keep the backdrop simple and allow the collection to take center stage. A long wooden bench, blue-rimmed glasses, and vases full of nodding sunflowers are all in keeping with the Southwest theme of the kitchen.

✵ ✵ ✵

OPPOSITE: Vibrant color and an inspired selection of Native art create a charming bar area in one corner of the kitchen. The sturdy cabinet of unpainted rubbed wood has been fitted with stunning stained glass panels that protect and display an array of Mexican-style barware. Below, handmade tiles in Southwest designs continue the colors and themes begun in stained glass, and a shallow ceramic basin dropped into the countertop serves as a small utility sink. Note that the sink's hardware and the light switches and electrical outlets have all been designed to blend tactfully into their dazzling surroundings.

❊ ❊ ❊

ABOVE: When designing your kitchen, think about the perspectives from other rooms. In this somewhat extreme example, the homeowner has decorated the tops of cabinets with tile mosaic and whimsical stuffed bulls, since the kitchen can be viewed from above through the gallery. Floor tiles also play an important role from this angle: these have been laid in various sizes and shapes, reminiscent of an oft-repaired cobblestone street.

❇ ❇ ❇

ABOVE: A loft kitchen carved out of raw space is defined by a screen of corrugated metal. This construction material's ability to follow curves and irregular spaces may make it a practical solution for you. Canary-colored walls and golden wood are juxtaposed against the glossy black of cabinet doors and appliances and the traditional, checker-board floor pattern. A triangle cutout opens onto blue sky.

ABOVE: A single nontraditional element can transform a room from boring to outrageous. The strong graphics of the inlaid floor save this plain space from being eminently forgettable. The geometrics of the tile reinforce the pattern of the quilted, diner-style, stainless steel backsplash, while bold primary colors coupled with black and white keep the design beautifully basic.

✖ ✖ ✖

OPPOSITE: A primary play space for preschoolers as well as a cooking and eating area for the young family, this kitchen accepts its role with humor and charm. In the "if you can't beat 'em, join 'em" spirit of decorating, the room's multipurpose function is celebrated with open areas of colorful tile, kids' drawings on the refrigerator, a downright funky glass-top table for dining, and a laminate-top drop-leaf table for messy children's projects. The walls and cabinets are painted with a glossy, wipe-clean paint so as to remain free of tiny fingerprints, and a half-wall shields diners from a view of the dirty dishes. The real beauty of this look is that it can be achieved with a minimum of expense: mismatched floor tile can be found at remnant sales (just be sure that all pieces are the same thickness); folding garden chairs are a snap to find—these have been painted in traditional nursery colors; and other fun furniture can be had at flea markets or secondhand shops.

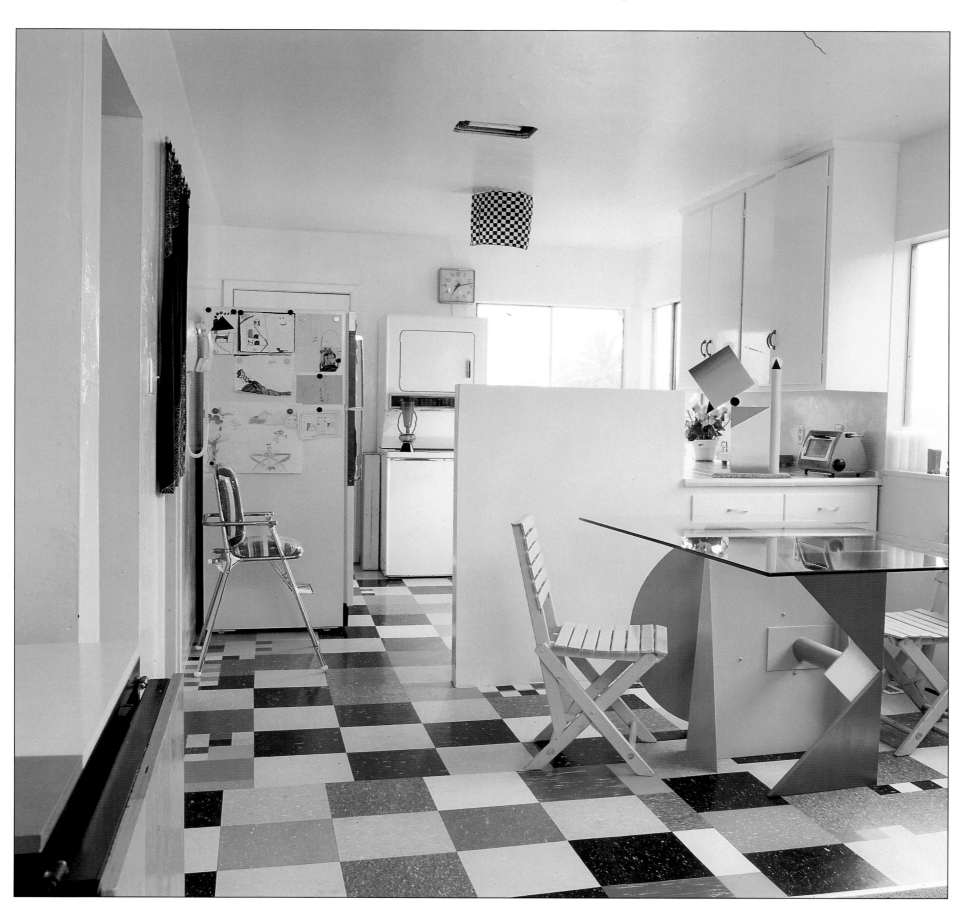

ABOVE: The ziggurat effect created by the underside of the stair treads adds a dramatic element to the kitchen area. Chairs covered with red laminate look like elaborate puzzle pieces, contributing to the playful feel of this modern room. The table surface is likewise covered with brightly colored laminate, which is echoed down the staircase and along the gallery above the table. A brilliant blue floor completes the triad of primary colors. Appliances in cool stainless steel appear to recede, allowing a sense of fun to rule.

❊ ❊ ❊

OPPOSITE: Inlaid linoleum in an irregular design looks more like a rug than like cold tile, yet it has all the ease of care that comes with linoleum. Flecks in the material add an attractive, textured quality, while stacks of brightly colored plates and mismatched porcelain knobs on cabinets and drawers pick up the floor's bold hues.

CHOOSING A STYLE

*D*eciding on a decor can be one of the trickier propositions in planning your kitchen. A bold design that strikes you as terrific in the store may grow tiresome when faced day after day—or worse, you may opt for a look that demands nearly impossible upkeep when kids, pets, and busy work schedules are factored in. Before you set your heart on a particular style, consider its disadvantages, and make sure that they're ones that you can live with.

In many cases, the prevailing style of the house will help you make many of your decisions: if the rest of the house is Colonial, a futuristic kitchen would be rather jarring. But even within a chosen style, there are many options available. Look through this book to get a sense of the possibilities, and mark the pages with kitchens that appeal to you. As you review the marked pages, you'll begin to see elements in common. Doubtless, you'll find many ideas to incorporate in your own kitchen. You'll make a safer choice if you let your decision "rest" for a couple of weeks. A new frame of mind may find you delighted with your choice or wavering somewhat; if you're uncertain now, you'll feel reassured that you haven't actually ordered anything yet.

Take a close look at your cooking habits, the daily traffic in your kitchen, and the amount of time you plan to devote to maintenance. Be realistic in your evaluations. If you are a working parent who hates to clean, then realize that the shining black and stainless steel surfaces that look so pristine on magazine pages will be marred by tiny (and probably not-so-tiny) fingerprints and cluttered with the normal (for most households) assortment of junk mail, lunch boxes, and school papers. If, on the other hand, you find cleaning cathartic or are single and rarely home for dinner, then that gorgeous sleek kitchen may work well for you.

Let your personality serve as a cue for your decor. The chief cook spends a lot of time in the kitchen, so it's only appropriate that the space reflect his or her tastes. If you love Southwestern pottery, consider making it your theme. Memorabilia—as well as textiles and dishware—from the thirties, forties, and fifties are another fun way to infuse a functional work space with personality. And kitchen collectibles from all eras are readily available and generally much less expensive than antiques for other rooms of the house. Search your attic for "heirlooms" that might have been overlooked; since the kitchen is an informal area, you can include pieces that are too casual for your other rooms. Old chairs, dressers, or tables can be stripped and painted or left as is to lend character and charm to your kitchen.

If you plan to decorate in a period style, you'll do well to be flexible. While the aura of the Victorian age is one of elegance and opulence, the practicality of kitchens of the day left much to be desired. Borrowing furniture styles, wallpaper designs, or window treatments to create an impression of the period will be enough for all but the most dedicated of historians. If, however, you object to the look of electrical appliances and other modern conveniences, you have some recourse. Many manufacturers provide appliances with an old-fashioned look; for instance, a refrigerator may take on the appearance of a wooden icebox or may have bead-board panels that allow it to disappear against a wall. Dishwashers and smaller appliances can often be hidden behind a panel or door. These valuable options allow you to preserve the look of the chosen period without sacrificing the conveniences of the twentieth century.

ABOVE: Simple ash cabinets stained in nontraditional colors impart the feel of an atelier in this roomy kitchen. The wall of windows and the handsome range hood add to the studio atmosphere. The absence of wall-hung cabinets creates an airy feel but is only practical because of the wealth of low cupboards and drawers.

✼ ✼ ✼

ABOVE: Sometimes a bold design also serves as a solution to a practical problem. A wedge removed from this glass-topped table allows it to slide smartly into place at the corner of the stainless steel island. Without this dramatic step, the table would crowd the space, or worse, there would be no room for an eating area at all. Instead, the creation becomes the centerpiece of the room, in both a design and a functional sense. Molded plastic chairs that curve to fit the body are perfect complements to the geometric lines of the other furnishings and the angular planes of the walls.

Chapter Three

Kitchens with Extras

In any remodeling project, the impulse to add something you've never had before can be nearly irresistible. Unfortunately, these impulses are sometimes squashed prematurely by what seems to be too small a space, or by a space that just doesn't seem to lend itself to that laundry area, desk, or play space you had in mind. Don't give up too soon; there may yet be a solution to your dilemma. Page through this chapter for inspiration on maximizing space and suggestions for compromises that will allow you to incorporate extras and to transform your kitchen from a simple cooking area to a supreme work space.

If the kitchen in your life is large enough, consider adding a desk. Here you can pay bills or set children to do homework without fear of tomato sauce appearing on the results. When you buy a new computer for the study, consider putting the old one in your kitchen work space (the heat and moisture of the kitchen can be damaging

to sensitive electronic equipment, so it isn't the best place for a state-of-the-art model). New computer software will not only keep track of recipes and balance your checkbook, but can also document your wine cellar, calculate nutritional values for recipes, and even play your favorite CDs.

Restaurant equipment is another extra worth considering if you're a serious cook: many manufacturers now produce professional-quality ranges that are designed for residences. For truly busy hostesses, two dishwashers can be a great addition to the kitchen; there's no need for loads of dirty plates to sit idle, waiting for the lone, hardworking dishwasher to be free.

Wine connoisseurs might wish to explore the possibilities of including space for wine storage in the kitchen, where it can be handy to the cooking and serving areas. Options range from expensive refrigerators with dual temperature control (one for red wine and one for white) to recessed "cellars" to simple racks.

ABOVE: A passion for collecting fine wines requires ingenuity when it comes to storage. Red wine should be stored at a steady, cool temperature, creating a challenge for owners of more than a few bottles. Here, empty space below the kitchen floor has been converted into a mini wine cellar; the hinged trapdoor is complete with a built-in ladder. Inventive storage bins act as insulation and protection for the bottles.

✖✖✖

OPPOSITE: The true wine lover's kitchen includes a professional wine refrigerator. Note the external gauges that effectively monitor temperature and light. Old-world charm permeates this space, affirming its identity as a favorite spot for informal tastings and complementing regular kitchen duties as well.

A separate pantry is a boon to those with large families, while laundry equipment in the kitchen can be a great timesaver, as a series of domestic chores can be staggered, all in one space. Models that stack, rather than sit side by side, are the most space efficient.

Nothing pleases the true gourmand more than herbs snipped fresh from the plant and tossed into a simmering dish. Windowsill gardens provide fresh herbs year-round and add a lovely homey touch as well. If you are truly green-thumbed and have the space, try growing vegetables indoors in containers or in special tables designed for hydroponics.

Set aside an area for play space and informal lunches if there are little ones in your life. You'll like being able to keep an eye on them and they'll appreciate the feeling of being at the center of things.

If part of your overall kitchen plan includes streamlining your work, adding to the pleasure you take in cooking, or encouraging family life, these little extras will lend terrific support your efforts.

✳ ✳ ✳

ABOVE: A planning desk with a cork backboard and mailbox slots above make this corner of the kitchen extremely functional. A narrow, vertical space that would otherwise go to waste has been converted into an innovative wine rack. The nearby cabinet stores glasses and other accessories.

❊ ❊ ❊

ABOVE: Creating a wine storage area on a lower level of a home or simply suggesting a cellar by the use of masonry brings a touch of Europe to the dining area. The wines are stored atop one another in wooden storage bins set into wall niches. Stone walls insulate the room, helping to keep the wine at a steady temperature.

ABOVE: This beautiful and somewhat formal kitchen has been outfitted with lavish materials worthy of a library. Cherry woodwork, brass hardware, and oriental rugs all contribute to the studylike ambience. And, indeed, a desk—complete with a computer—helps make short work of shopping lists, banking tasks, and myriad other chores.

❊ ❊ ❊

OPPOSITE: This carefully planned work space has been designed to blend seamlessly with the design of the kitchen while gently harboring a miniature office. The elongated desk, which matches kitchen cabinetry, boasts utility drawers, two file drawers, and room for a telephone. The wicker desk chair, in keeping with the informality of a kitchen, is airier than most office furniture and yet looks natural against the surrounding deep wood tones.

ABOVE: The similarly curving lines of desk and peninsula serve to unite this wide-open multipurpose space. Matching chairs at dining table, breakfast bar, and desk as well as the shared surfaces on countertops and floor also help to pull the space together. A gallery of carefully placed black-and-white photographs tames the disorder of the desk below, while the corkboard above the desktop further organizes receipts, phone messages, and other bits of office paper.

❈ ❈ ❈

OPPOSITE: Generous counter space allows room for a computer/word processor, which saves countless hours in record-keeping and provides quick access to recipe files. Computer hardware and the ultramodern shape of the peninsula are juxtaposed with the old-world arch of the window, but these disparate elements are united by the cinnamon color of walls and floor.

ABOVE LEFT: Perfectly at home in this modern space, the television becomes a design feature as well as a practical one in this loft kitchen. The entertainment center is built into the room divider, preserving the sleek look of the space; cabinet doors above and below the television hide the clutter of interior shelves.

✕ ✕ ✕

ABOVE RIGHT: A state-of-the-art entertainment center is positioned near the kitchen seating area for easy access. Music helps the cook pass the time, and the kitchen bar stools can be turned to watch television during a quiet cup of coffee. A sliding door hides all when the equipment is not in use.

✕ ✕ ✕

OPPOSITE: This fortuitous kitchen arrangement—with the stove and plenty of counter space facing the television—is well suited to a self-paced cooking course, taught via television program or videocassette tape. The large screen is in its element in this high-tech environment, and is also positioned for more relaxed viewing from the living room.

ABOVE: Convenient laundry space has been carved out of an empty wall in this country kitchen. A front-loading washer and dryer are concealed behind sliding cabinet doors. Alongside the appliances are hamper drawers and a handy utility drawer, while cupboards above store a plethora of detergents, stain removers, and fabric softeners. Note the narrow closet door beside the window, which hides a fold-down ironing board.

OPPOSITE: A kitchen tucked into the corner of a barn makes room for a washer and dryer on the same wall as other water-consuming appliances—the sink and the dishwasher. This is an important consideration when factoring in installation and plumbing costs, since close proximity to existing pipes prevents you from having to lay new water lines.

ABOVE: A tiny desk tucked into the corner of the kitchen is a prized playspace for any young child. Here, a thrift shop desk is paired with a little wooden chair; the ruffled flounce and chintz cushion give the seat a decidedly feminine air. Corkboard framed with painted strips of stock molding relieves the refrigerator of its duty as a juvenile art gallery, while a sweetly papered toy trunk hides a jumble of playthings.

OPPOSITE: Families with several children must often adapt the kitchen in order to accommodate the needs of the little ones. This modular play unit, which matches the counter and cabinetry of the kitchen proper, occupies a corner that might otherwise be used as an informal dining area. Here, the kids can keep busy as parents prepare for dinner. It's also a great place to serve the children breakfast and lunch. Quarter-circle wedges, at just the right height for junior seating, retreat into the module on easy-glide casters. The wipe-clean surfaces and bright colors add to this kitchen's practical and cheerful persona.

ABOVE: A hydroponic vegetable garden keeps fresh fruits and vegetables within arm's length year-round. Vining plants will climb a support, such as the rafters shown here, to become a strong design element as well as lunch. The proper exposure, the right types of plants, and good growing conditions are essential for successful indoor gardening. This custom-made growing table has a slotted floor for drainage and controls for regulating heat and light.

THE INDOOR HERB GARDEN

A favorite kitchen extra is a potted herb garden, which will supply you with fresh herbs throughout the year, as well as the much-desired element of greenery—and some even offer showy flowers. Herbs will grow happily indoors if their not-inconsequential demands are met.

▦ Plant your herbs in pots that are large enough to accomodate the plants' roots. If the roots are crowded, your herbs will founder. Provide the rich, well-drained soil that herbs love by using a good commercial potting mixture.

▦ Herbs grown indoors need lots of direct sunlight—at least five hours a day for most, although a few (mint, parsely, rosemary, and thyme) prefer partial shade. If your kitchen doesn't receive this quantity of natural light, you can use a fluorescent bulb or a grow-light, sold at most garden centers, to supplement sunlight. You'll need to leave the grow-light on for approximately fifteen hours a day to fully replace direct sunlight; make sure to place the bulb well above plants—6 to 8 inches (15 to 20cm)—or risk burning their delicate leaves.

▦ Water the herbs whenever the surface of the soil begins to feel dry. Since a container is a relatively small growing space, this may even be every day. Make sure, though, not to overwater the plants: saturated soil and pots sitting in water promote a condition called root rot. Also, plants will be grateful for room-temperature water; cool tap water can be a shock to their sensitive systems.

▦ You'll also need to feed your herbs. Visit your local garden center and pick up some fish emulsion or seaweed. To ensure luxurious growth, feed herbs once a month with one of these natural fertilizers mixed at half-strength.

▦ Herbs prefer a cooler temperature than humans—60° to 65° F (16° to 18° C)—so a windowsill is a good setting for your indoor herb garden, though plants should not be placed too close to freezing window panes. Nor should they be exposed to strong drafts (though they do like gently circulating air), so if your windows let in blasts of cold air in winter, you'd do best to find another area of the kitchen for your herbs.

▦ Occasionally, herbs grown indoors will become infested with spider mites, whiteflies, or aphids. This is usually brought on by the warm, dry air in most homes. If you notice tiny insects on your plants, first isolate the affected plants in an area well away from other houseplants. Then spray plants with a solution of warm water and soap—2 tablespoons of mild, flaked soap to 1 gallon (4L) of water—every three days until signs of infestation disappear. Even when plants look healthy again, check beneath the leaves for insects, as eggs can continue to hatch for several weeks. Be sure to rinse soap-treated leaves well before adding them to food!

▦ Basil, chervil, chives, lemon balm, mint, oregano, parsley, rosemary, sage, sweet marjoram, tarragon, and thyme are all good culinary herbs for growing indoors. In addition to cooking, many of them can be used in herbal teas, flavored oils and vinegars, potpourri, and even floral arrangements. Be creative with your newfound source of fresh herbs.

ABOVE: A sunny southern or western exposure will aid your windowsill gardening efforts. Here, a lush crop of miniature citrus, rosemary, and other herbs waits near an array of spices and oils to be added to the evening meal. The tiny garden's proximity to the sink helps create the warmth and humidity of a greenhouse climate.

ABOVE: An ingenious system, designed in Italy, combines an exhaust function, a light source, and even a plate rack for quick-drying dishes fresh from the sink below. Professional-quality equipment such as this, together with the superior cookware and fresh ingredients stored efficiently in nearby cabinets and refrigerator, creates a kitchen paradise for those devoted to the culinary arts. Pots of herbs grace shelves, imparting a measure of Italian country spirit and ensuring that each delectable dish tastes its freshest.

❈ ❈ ❈

OPPOSITE: A kitchen in a greenhouse bump-out can be an inspiring setting for daily chores or informal gatherings. Air conditioning and low-e windows that screen the sun's heating rays make a room with myriad windows comfortable even in the middle of summer. Cabinets and appliances, including a professional undercounter refrigerator/freezer, are set low to the ground to leave the view unobstructed. Ventilation for the professional range is custom down-drafted to avoid unsightly risers against the glass wall. Pots of flowers suspended from wrought-iron plant hangers keep the view in bloom even when harsh winter weather hits.

※ ※ ※

ABOVE: Natural birch, stainless steel, and black matte Formica offer a level of sophistication that matches the professional equipment found in this wonderfully outfitted kitchen. The professional range top drops conveniently into a standard-depth cabinet. Warming trays below the oven make the timing of intricate meals a breeze. The stainless steel worktable—a stock unit—rolls on casters and is infinitely practical in this small space. It can move where it's needed or be pushed out of the way, whereas a chunky, stationary island might actually inhibit the flow of work.

ABOVE: Its monochromatic palette and grid shapes reminiscent of shoji screens imbue this kitchen with an oriental serenity. The movable serving table is a practical addition, used to trundle dishes and serving pieces to the dining room and back. When not in use, the cart's flip-top, accordion design allows it to fold easily for storage in even a slim space such as a broom closet. Royal blue trays and shining chrome add flair to any decor.

✳✳✳

ABOVE: A professional range, with its eight burners and two ovens, stands ready to prepare prodigious quantities of food. An army of stockpots, at attention on the low shelf of a sturdy and spacious island, promises to lend a hand. The range and hood boast space-saving features, such as a stainless steel shelf for storing oils and spices and a multitude of hooks for organizing cooking utensils.

ABOVE: Professional medical stainless steel and glass cabinets line the walls in a gleaming display of efficiency. The clean, simple lines are a fitting backdrop for the organic forms of the fruits and vegetables that naturally grace kitchen counters.

Chapter Four

Eating Areas and Adjoining Spaces

Many of today's kitchens also serve as dining spaces or are part of a larger living area. This places additional responsibility on the kitchen: it must be a comfortable, serene dining area as well as a practical work space. Whether your kitchen's eating area offers the only table in the house or simply complements a separate dining room, there are dozens of possibilites for carving out seating that will satisfy your needs.

The tiniest kitchen may allow only a perch and two stools, while a roomy kitchen will happily accommodate a hulking farm table and eight chairs. If your kitchen is too small to seat the requisite number and your home lacks a proper dining room, look to the foyer, the family room, or a part of the living room to create an eating arrangement with the area and the ambience you want.

Combining the family room with the kitchen is a great way to invite the whole family to spend more time together. The extended space allows for relaxing and sharing the news of the day as meals are cooked, eaten, and cleaned up, all in the cozy setting of a room designed specifically for encouraging family sharing. Half-height room dividers, or "stub walls," can define the kitchen area of your great room, and will turn your kitchen around a bit so that all the work surfaces needn't be against the walls. Locating the sink, cooktop, and/or counter midroom allows the clan chef to chat comfortably as he or she chops ingredients, cooks dinner, and rinses the dishes.

Color, light, and texture can help you tie together the spaces you have annexed to your kitchen or, in the case of an open plan, will allow you to effectively marry the kitchen to the living room. There is a delicate balance to be achieved in combining spaces, no matter

ABOVE: This coolly sophisticated dining space with open kitchen is designed for informal entertaining. Guests may visit with the cook as he or she prepares the feast; the long shelf, supported by shining columns, functions as a sideboard for buffets or host serving.

OPPOSITE: French doors lead to a scenic balcony set for alfresco dining. The rustic atmosphere of the kitchen—with its heavy beams, roughly planked walls, and brick floor—is a perfect foil for the adjoining outdoor room. Undressed doors allow light to stream through; on balmy days the doors can be left ajar for a summery, country feeling. New white cabinetry keeps the paneled ceiling and walls from appearing overbearing and tempers the woodsy feeling.

what the characters of the spaces involved. The areas should be distinct yet observing of a certain sense of continuity. If your kitchen and living areas employ different color schemes, a uniform floor treatment throughout the joined space will declare them related; if, on the other hand, the rooms have a common hue, a tiled floor area or a rug can define a separate eating area. Often, a few elements— like a fabric pattern, pieces of a collection, or touches of a single color—carried from one space to the other are enough to create a coherent design.

Remember that in an open plan, good ventilation in the cooking area is key. Delectable aromas can quickly turn into sour odors if they're not whisked away by briskly circulating air. A vented overhead or undercounter system is ideal, and should be calibrated to the BTUs of your burners and any other cooking equipment

you use, such as a grill, wok stove, or countertop broiler. Also available are small air purifiers that simply plug into an electrical outlet and cleanse the air of food particles, cigarette smoke, and airborne dust.

If you should be lucky enough to have a terrace, balcony, porch, or patio, appropriate the area for warm-weather dining. Setting a table out-of-doors adds a wonderful dimension to the dining experience and effectively gains you an extra room.

Train your eye to look for the infinite possibilities for creating comfortable eating areas and annexing nearby niches in your kitchen, and you'll open yourself up to the joys of found space. Once you've discovered a way to incorporate seating into your kitchen plan, let your imagination guide you in creating the perfect dining spot for your needs.

ABOVE: A corner of square panes assures a sunny disposition in this informal eating space. No window treatment can be the best window treatment for a framed view with character—consider leaving windows bare unless privacy is an issue. Colonial green tile, white paint, and honey-hued chairs combine well with the quaint old stove and the quietly genteel glassware.

✳✳✳

OPPOSITE LEFT: A stair step or two is a good way to separate adjoined but distinct areas—if you are designing your kitchen from scratch, you may wish to consider this as an option. Here, a wire-backed chair reminiscent of those found in old ice cream parlors resides with a tiny table just below the kitchen. The sunny space is protected by a plaid pull-up shade; an identical shade in the kitchen links the two areas. Both the decorative tray affixed to the side of the dishwasher and the ornamental cabbage plant help to define the spaces.

✳✳✳

OPPOSITE RIGHT: A round table in golden oak and four matched chairs look completely at home in this airy kitchen. A more formal set might overwhelm the space or appear discordant, but this traditional country design harmonizes well with the simple white cabinetry and chintz window treatments.

ABOVE LEFT: A café-height round table and two upholstered stools provide a small but comfortable space for breakfast or evening coffee. Poised just outside the kitchen proper, the tiny eating area enjoys a view of the landscaped terrace beyond the back door.

❈ ❈ ❈

ABOVE RIGHT: A peaceful breakfast nook combines Victorian furniture and decorative objects with contemporary patterns for a fresh but formal look. Wrought iron and marble rest between a pair of vintage chairs dressed in new upholstery. Striped swags complement walls covered with black polka dots. Greenery and two framed nineteenth-century botanical prints finish off the simple space.

❈ ❈ ❈

OPPOSITE: In a loft, a separate area can be created using the power of suggestion. With a simple change in the texture of the floor, a dining room emerges. Here, the transition from tile to pine produces an island of eating space. The hanging lamp centered over the table reinforces the sense of the dining area as a room unto itself.

❊❊❊

ABOVE: A brick fireplace with a raised hearth imparts Colonial charm in this large kitchen space. The fire brings a warm glow to the gleaming wood of the bare tabletop, while festive flowered plates and forced bulbs hint at the promise of spring despite the leafless tree outside the window.

ABOVE: Built-in bookcases, a table and two chairs in dark wood, and a wainscoted, muraled wall create the ambience of a library. The silver coffee service and a bowl of roses add to the elegance in this traditional setting.

ABOVE: A half-height, wainscoted room divider copies the wholesome look of a country fence, complete with newel post. The partition allows the cook to chat with guests, but shields diners from a view of the kitchen once all are seated. Wainscoting is repeated on the cupboard door below the sink, and a leafy William Morris wallpaper runs through both rooms behind the half-wall. The rooms are further defined by overhead beams that effectively but subtly quarter the room.

OPPOSITE: This cozy Victorian kitchen boasts enough space for a defined eating area. The painted open cupboard, turned-leg table, and upholstered chairs offer a sense of comfort traditionally found in the dining room. Positioned squarely over the table, a brass lighting fixture with frosted glass globes helps to separate the eating space by asserting that the table is indeed the center of a "room." Decorative objects and bowls of fresh fruit along the peninsula ease the transition from the working nature of the kitchen to the relaxing atmosphere of the eating area.

✳✳✳

ABOVE: Formal touches imbue this eat-in kitchen with a sturdy elegance. Antique trays grace lemon yellow walls, a unique backdrop for handsome pine cabinetry. An elaborate chandelier fitted with bare bulbs hangs high above the wide-plank table. Note that the pricey pieces—the dishware and the chandelier—have been placed well out of the way of daily traffic.

DINING ALFRESCO

Alfresco is a combination of two Italian words and means, literally, "in the cool"—outdoors, away from the accumulated heat of the day and the fuss and bother of the kitchen. Although most homes today are air-conditioned, eliminating the need to escape to the once-cooler terrace, there's still a special place in our hearts for the joys of dining out-of-doors. If you have a porch, patio, terrace, or balcony where you can set a table, consider yourself lucky and take full advantage of this magical space by planning brunches, afternoon teas, and extravagant dinners surrounded by the peace and beauty of nature.

The type of furniture you choose for your alfresco meals will depend on several factors. You must first consider how much space you have; whether it is sheltered by a roof; how much you can spend on furnishings; and whether the furniture will have a permanent place outdoors and, if so, whether it will remain in place year-round. Your outdoor accomodations can be as elaborate as a full set of cast-iron chairs and matching table or as impromptu as a card table draped with a lovely tablecloth. Make sure that the furniture you choose is sufficiently weatherproof for your situation: for instance, iron (if it is painted regularly to deter rust), aluminum, and treated woods are good choices for furniture that must remain outdoors year-round; wicker is a lovely material if your space is sheltered from harsh weather. If you plan to move table and chairs outdoors as needed, opt for light pieces that can be stored out of the way. A trestle table that can be easily broken down after each use and stored flat is an ideal candidate; pick up mismatched secondhand chairs at flea markets and yard sales for eclectic, inexpensive seating, or choose folding garden chairs, which are available in an array of handsome colors.

Dining outdoors needn't mean paper plates, plastic forks, and flyaway napkins. Bring out your best when you entertain alfresco—china, silverware, and damask napkins stay where they're put and are infinitely more festive. Or, if you fear for your cherished place settings, consider purchasing an outdoor set of dishes in heavy plastic, now being made in gorgeous jewel tones. Keep plenty of trays and baskets handy to help transport goods to the table; if you have no stairs to contend with, a butler's cart saves countless steps. To prevent the tablecloth from blowing up in a gust, buy tablecloths with specially weighted edges or adapt your own tablecloths by tacking weights to the bottom of favorite table linens.

If too-close neighbors are a problem, think about erecting a privacy fence. This fence needn't encircle your entire property for you to get the privacy you need for dining; often, just a few yards is enough to create the retreat you need. A well-placed trellis or latticework screen is also an effective barrier. Once lush vines and climbers fill in, you'll have a private oasis that is more fluid than a fence. While a mature hedge also creates adequate privacy, you may not be willing to wait for it to grow to a useful height. Instead, potted trees—already grown to an appropriate height—can be arranged in a row to provide proper seclusion.

Don't forget the charms of evening dining. Balmy breezes, flickering starlight, and the fragrance of blooming roses can create an enchanting scene, though the picture is easily marred by mosquitoes. Citronella candles will provide romantic lighting as well as a deterrent to these vicious pests. If your dining space is not too vast and the guest list not too large, consider tenting mosquito netting around the table. Not only will it keep biting insects out, it will infuse the setting with an exotic aura.

ABOVE: Step out onto the porch for a breezy lunch. Italian dishware and heavy, cobalt-rimmed glasses create a setting that is both practical and festive. Place mats are beautiful and effectively shield the table but don't blow in the wind as readily as tablecloths. On lazy afternoons, there's nothing better than enjoying the fresh tastes of summer in a sunny outdoor space.

ABOVE: An out-of-the-way corner of the kitchen has been transformed into a "breakfast room" with very little effort. A coffeepot, bean grinder, and toaster share the wide shelf with jars of dried pasta and other kitchen necessities. A collection of whimsical teapots and a well-loved teddy bear ease family members into the day; the morning paper waits in a nearby basket. Stripes, plaids, and dots mix cheerfully in a pleasant wake-up call.

❊ ❊ ❊

OPPOSITE: This kitchen/dining area is roomy enough to include a cozy sitting area before the tile fireplace. Rockers dressed in country quilts, a coffee table, and traditional lamps bring the ambience of a living room into the kitchen. White paneling on the walls and ceiling, combined with plenty of natural light from uncovered windows and the French door, keep dark wood and unorthodox furnishings from overburdening this spacious kitchen.

❆ ❆ ❆

ABOVE: This room was designed for a family that lives in the kitchen. The time-worn table welcomes plenty of visitors. A platform-style couch upholstered in a Native American pattern provides a comfy spot where guests can visit with the host or a weary cook can relax and await the outcome of a new culinary endeavor. Desk space for keeping household accounts or supervising children's homework is close at hand, but preserves the look of a kitchen area rather than a study by echoing the functional white of the kitchen cabinets. Ceramic bowls ornament the desktop instead of the traditional pencils and paperweights. Subtle lengths of turquoise—used for the backsplash, the matching tile below the couch, and the door frame—unify the vast space.

❋❋❋

ABOVE: This kitchen/dining area division is typical of many suburban homes. Though there is a partial wall and separate floor treatments, each room provides a full view of the other, so it's preferable that the areas be compatible in terms of design. Side chairs waiting against the cabinet divider are technically in the kitchen; this property of the dining area serves to unite the two spaces. The Welsh cupboard set against the dining room wall echoes the counter and open shelves on the same wall of the kitchen. Splashy floral fabric graces the dining table and chairs and also decks the kitchen shelves, cementing the visual link between these complementary spaces.

ABOVE: A kitchen in an old barn melds seamlessly with the living area through careful choice of materials. The stucco-faced island, which efficiently houses sink, dishwasher, and cabinets, backs right up to the couch. The island's maple top complements the warm tones of wooden beams and Southwest colors. Curving walls, island, and archway lend a fluid, easygoing atmosphere. Given the same treatment as the surrounding walls—which have been ragged a glowing claret color—a built-in refrigerator becomes a modern armoire.

OPPOSITE: Strategic placement of a couch separates living room from kitchen/eating area in this airy studio space. White, glass-front cabinets keep storage looking light and bright, reducing the kitcheny quality of the cupboards. Black mesh chairs pulled up to a marble-top island provide all the eating space an on-the-go individual requires.

✠ ✠ ✠

ABOVE: The long harvest table bridges the kitchen and living areas, while pine plank walls and flooring offer breezy continuity. The nearly exclusive use of white defines the tiny but efficient kitchen and brightens the entire area. A vaulted ceiling relieves the boxiness of the room, making the relatively small cabin seem intimate rather than cramped. Bold buffalo check and a subtle red, white, and blue theme contribute casual charm to this delightful mountain retreat.

✻✻✻

ABOVE: A half-wall, painted a striking garnet and draped with an Indian blanket, hides kitchen clutter and creates a serene backdrop for the lavishly pillowed couch. Folk art and fresh vegetables perch atop the wall, acknowledging the mixed use of the space. Spots of red in the kitchen—on spatterware bowls and coffeepot as well as old-fashioned tins—pick up on the red hues of the living area. A rustic note predominates throughout, though the room is no less polished than a more formal kitchen/living room.

Chapter Five

Dream Kitchens

Travel the primrose path to kitchens that present a full complement of solutions. In the dazzling kitchens that follow, space was not an issue and compromises only rarely had to be made. While few of us are in this enviable position, we can learn much from those who are. Strict duplication of these results might be impractical, but judicious borrowing of concepts and solutions can truly lead to the kitchen of your dreams.

There are a few general principles that apply to all good kitchens, no matter what their size. First, finding the right place for all your equipment will automatically create order and space. From a well-organized kitchen, large or small, efficiency and beauty naturally flow.

Another good rule is to research well the variety of options open to you. While you probably won't be able to indulge all your fantasies,

start out with a list of your ultimate desires and then begin collecting information about those particular features. Once you've discovered the uses, benefits, and costs of each of these elements, you'll be able to make informed decisions about which ones you can reasonably include in your plan.

In this chapter we'll also explore kitchen areas that take full advantage of architectural gifts. Vaulted ceilings, soaring pillars, and massive fireplaces are not the norm in every home, but they may be one of the selling points of your kitchen—or maybe they're features on your fantasy list that you may just go ahead and add!

In today's global culture, we've all learned to adapt from different societies elements that seem to work, from politics to fashion. This practice is no less true in the world of kitchen design. Interesting designs from England soften a high-efficiency approach with an

ABOVE: A dramatic carved arch sets off the frieze and ceiling molding in this beautifully spare kitchen. The usual island is foregone for an elegant worktable, whose legs, in contrast to the solid block of an island, impart an airy feel to the room. The stained floor border around the work space creates the illusion of a rug without the worry of cleaning one. Colorwashed cabinets in a buttermilk shade allow the beauty of the wood to show through while providing a creamy tone. A Craftsman-style lamp is both distinctive and understated. The entire room embodies the restraint and pride of design that were hallmarks of the Arts and Crafts Movement.

❋ ❋ ❋

OPPOSITE: A graceful curve of classically crafted cherry cabinets dominates this open kitchen space. Ceiling beams carry the warmth of wood to the rest of the house. Two semicircles of muted gray tile—on counter and floor—are practical in the preparation area; wooden planking keeps the balance of the floor both beautiful and comfortable to walk on. The wall of windows and several squared columns are all the accent this room needs.

acknowledged need for comfort, which extends as far as placing a wing chair and reading lamp in a corner of the kitchen. High-tech Italian designs provide drama and incredible efficiency, tempered with wit and an eccentric use of color.

As you plan your kitchen, consider the points of view of all members of your family. An exceptionally tall cook who likes to stir-fry may want a chopping surface at his or her height; the baker in the family might appreciate a marble-topped island for creating delectable

pastries. Integrate their wishes with your own to arrive at a genuine family space.

The ability to translate these fantasies into reality is what the chapter on dream kitchens is all about. Gather your clippings, notes, and catalogs and review them carefully. Listen to your instincts about color, style, shape, and equipment size. Assimilating all your research into one thoughful plan will deliver a well-designed, efficient, beautiful space that is sure to fit your very own definition of a dream kitchen.

ABOVE LEFT: This is truly a kitchen to dream about. The luxury of two islands promises all the preparation space any cook could want, while double ovens, a well-stocked pot rack, and a professional range back up that promise, delivering deluxe equipment to match. Wire racks on the tile backsplash above the sink hold additional accessories in a stunning display of efficiency.

✖ ✖ ✖

ABOVE RIGHT: Space is not an issue in this glorious kitchen; there is plenty of elbow room for a whole contingent of cooks. Parquet flooring laid in a herringbone pattern contributes visual interest to the wide open space. The Garland stove, trio of sinks, and vast counter and storage areas mark this as a kitchen designed for a serious cook. Angled for convenience, the peninsula breaks the squareness of the room and separates the kitchen proper from the adjacent dining area. Classic white cabinetry and gleaming counters combine with a delicate fruit motif in a refined and traditional kitchen.

❈ ❈ ❈

ABOVE: This wonderful apartment kitchen is a marvel of efficiency. Though square footage is slight, amenities are not. Undermounted sinks are surrounded by granite counters that feature an integral, carved drainboard. A railing mounted at the counter's edge is repeated on the backsplash, where it holds all manner of utensils and even accommodates a small wire shelf and propped bowls. The black finish on the range and the onyx tone of utility drawers complement sleek gray cabinets and shining steel fittings. On the hanging lamp, a trio of glass discs echoes the slivers of shelving above the range.

ARCHITECTURAL DETAILS

*A*rchitectural details are some of the most stunning additions to any kitchen. Perhaps your kitchen is already blessed with graceful crown moldings, fluted columns, or etched glass windows. If so, rejoice and give them prominence. It's likely, though, that your room is absent of any distinctive architectural detail. Don't despair; you can add singular details that impart character and elegance in your kitchen.

⊞ Depending on what you have in mind, decorating with architectural details can be rather complicated or quite simple. Stock moldings in a range of styles are available at hardware stores and home centers, and are relatively easy to add around the perimeter of the ceiling. A single stained glass window contributes color and gently filters light, and can be installed by a local glazier. Heavy pieces like stone gargoyles that you plan to set into a wall are best left to a professional mason, who will know how best to mount the material and will have on hand the special tools to hold it in place until the mortar is secure.

⊞ In addition to calling on retailers and manufacturers that produce new fixtures and trims, explore the intriguing world of architectural salvage. Most large cities have salvage warehouses or yards; auctions and flea markets are another good source for recyclable pieces. Be creative in the ways you use these found objects: pieces that were originally intended for exterior use, such as garden gates or door transoms, can often find a new life indoors as wall art. Mantelpieces, cut to an appropriate size, can create inspired shelving, and sawed-off columns can support tables or shelves. Let your imagination be your only limit and the result will be a room with a personality as unique as your own.

⊞ Don't overlook small pieces. While massive mantels and pillars are the most dramatic, careful attention to tiny details can create a room that is just as magnificent. Antique doorknobs, vintage faucets, and old-fashioned cabinet and drawer pulls can be found at flea markets and yard sales as well as antique shops and architectectural salvage emporiums, and are much more affordable than large pieces. Just a few of these beautifully crafted details thoughtfully placed can create an overall impression of warmth and charm.

⊞ Before you install vintage plumbing or decades-old light fixtures, have the pieces checked out by a licensed tradesman, who will be able to point out potential problems with leaks or any dubious wiring. Even if the hardware or lamp looks fairly decrepit, the piece can often be brought up to the appropriate safety standards.

⊞ Highlight architectural details by tailoring your paint scheme to the particular feature. Columns, moldings, and other trimwork stand out against a backdrop of color when they're treated to a coat of lustrous white paint. Or leave woodwork in its natural unpainted state but polish it to a high gloss in order to attract maximum attention. If you prefer a rustic look, leave your treasure untouched, but be sure to create a pristine setting to show your find to full advantage. Ancient-looking stone details take on a modern twist when surrounding walls are painted vibrant hues like scarlet or amethyst. For a more classic approach, bathe walls in shades of white or cream.

ABOVE: Vaulted ceilings endow a room with special charm. Handsome custom cabinetry, fitted with nautical hardware, allows cupboards of a size that suit the cook's personal taste and kitchenware collection. Custom work also permits special features, such as the warming drawer below the microwave oven, to be matched to cabinet facing. Stone flooring, elegant iron chairs, and a ceramic tile backsplash with angels contribute to the opulent air of the room.

ABOVE: Necessary ceiling support becomes a distinct advantage when given a sculptural look. The contrast of redwood stained cabinets with light ones is a dramatic touch that is pulled off with the help of a tile frieze stationed between upper and lower cupboards. This colorful band marries the disparate elements while providing a subtle focus for the eye. Black drawer knobs, counter edgings, and random floor tiles punctuate expanses of pale color. An array of lighting choices also helps make this kitchen something special: plate glass windows and several skylights let in streams of natural light; mini fluorescent rings provide overall illumination; and pendant lamps reminiscent of trumpet flowers direct light on specific tasks.

❈❈❈

ABOVE: The heart of this informal home, the cozy kitchen allows family members to spread out and make themselves comfortable. The well-worn table and chairs are close enough to the cooking area for visitors to sit and enjoy a glass of wine while chatting with the cook. Though the kitchen is large, its warm wood floors, Shaker-style appointments, and folk art accents make it a homey, down-to-earth spot.

❀❀❀

ABOVE: The ambience of an old-fashioned country store permeates this beautiful and efficient kitchen. The double oven, with a heat-resistant low counter set before it, coupled with a range top on the island offers additional comforts to the serious cook. Glass-front refrigerated bins, each with its own temperature control, store bulky fruits and vegetables that might otherwise crowd the refrigerator. A homey brick fireplace, niche shelving, and a quaint desk increase the charm of this spacious yet cozy kitchen.

ABOVE: An exuberant use of color enlivens an otherwise traditional country kitchen. Deep mossy green has been applied to produce a textural effect on walls, while bead-board paneling and the raftered ceiling have been coated in a creamy white. Hanging lamps with emerald glass shades march around the perimeter of the vast, maple-topped island, supplementing the natural light from windows and skylight. An enormous range hood, balanced by the bulk of the island, creates the effect of an awning at the far end of the room. Note the placement of sinks: one, just steps from the stove, is convenient for filling pasta pots or adding water to simmering dishes; the other is set into the island, and waits patiently for vegetables to be washed or for dishes to be soaked and then loaded into the nearby dishwasher. Decorative touches like the antique plates atop the professional refrigerator and the garland of fragrant bay leaves draping the clock are the hallmark of a comfy kitchen.

✖ ✖ ✖

OPPOSITE: Words from the worldly wise stenciled onto walls and floorcloth personalize this room in a way that is bold yet distinguished. Colorful cubist designs or funky modern sculpture would look out of place with the traditional paneling, fieldstone fireplace, and pine cabinetry, but the flowing calligraphy and illustrious quotations provide witty and stylish decoration. The room is spacious enough to accommodate two tables—one generally used as a worktable, the other set for dining. When necessary, however, the two can be pushed together to take on a joint role as either work surface or dining table. This pot rack functions more like a shelf, keeping equipment up and out of the way.

"If You ~~[Are]~~
Invite~~[d]~~
Obl~~[ige]~~ ~~[Pleasing]~~."
—The Duchess of Windsor

"I Will Not Eat Oysters. I Want My Food Dead—Not Sick, Not Wounded—"

POST

�֎ �֎ �֎

ABOVE: A spectacular view lends a touch of magic to any room. This rustic Southwest kitchen benefits from breathtaking scenery as well as a clear sense of style. A three-sided adobe fireplace throws light into the living room as it warms the kitchen on chilly nights. Natural colors are in keeping with the expansive view, and touches like the counter's small rock shelf and the collection of eggs extend the nature theme.

❆❆❆

ABOVE: This large contemporary kitchen is pleasing in its spareness, avoiding the uninhabited feeling of many minimalist decors. High-ceilinged rooms often suffer from a sense of emptiness in the upper region of the space; here, that vacant look is eliminated with a cutout, a niche, and a shelf all constructed in the top half of the kitchen. The niche and shelf are filled with Southwestern pottery, which mixes well with the simple Shaker design of the furniture. Stacked wall ovens, a state-of-the-art range top, an enormous built-in refrigerator, and a roomy appliance garage that hides a coffeemaker and food processor all add to the desirability of this dreamy kitchen.

ABOVE: An open kitchen/dining room doesn't have to be casual. Wooden floors polished to a high shine combine with Classical architectural details in a design that breathes an air of formality. Walls and ceiling have been painted a flat eggshell, while columns, cornices, and cupboards are treated to a paler, glossy paint. This trick quietly draws attention to these accents and introduces a subtle tone-on-tone effect. A generous island, which also incorporates stately columns, offers a practical work surface as well as plenty of additional storage. Elegant Windsor chairs, a Colonial-style iron chandelier, and an antique Welsh cupboard filled with collectible Spode augment the formal atmosphere that in the past would have been reserved for a proper dining room.

❊ ❊ ❊

ABOVE: This wonderfully commodious kitchen designed for serious cooks is the height of practicality, and its bright cheerfulness makes kitchen chores a pleasure. The unique multilevel island has two platforms that allow a cookbook stand to be set at eye level or provide space for extra ingredients to be set out of the way of accidents. Two glass-shaded lamps offer task lighting above the work space, complementing the recessed bulbs that shed more diffuse light. A professional range and the battery of cookware hanging from the sturdy pot rack testify to the talents of this kitchen's inhabitants. Traditional checkerboard tiles in an expansive backsplash get updated with strips of gray defining squares that resemble quilt blocks. The polished wood floor, matching ceiling moldings, and glass-front cabinets that can be opened from either side provide continuity between the kitchen and the adjoining breakfast room.

ABOVE LEFT: Cooking area, dining space, and breakfast nook are combined in this dreamy, sunlit kitchen. White walls and cabinetry, along with an open design and soaring columns, keep the space light and airy; black counters and chairs ground the room. But while the chairs are dark-colored, the woven seats and slatted backs with central cutouts impart a suitably delicate touch. A low counter set along the room divider allows dining-height chairs to sidle up for breakfast or a quick lunch. These extra chairs stand ready to be added to the table when company arrives. A mural along the backsplash paints in leafy plants, and plenty of flowers and greenery add their freshness to the room.

✽✽✽

ABOVE RIGHT: A certain rustic quality survives despite the wealth of electrical appliances in this extremely well-appointed kitchen. Oak cabinetry and unfinished beams offset the technology boom so much in evidence: burners and a grill are set into the tiled countertop; large state-of-the-art refrigerators grace the far wall; a sleek European oven and a television take their places beside cabinets; not one, but two, dishwashers flank the island face; and there's even a computer, which can be concealed behind the tambour door in order to protect it from the heat and moisture of the kitchen. Reflecting the somewhat eccentric personality of the owner, a tomato red sink is set into the island, across from a full-size commercial popcorn machine!

✽✽✽

OPPOSITE: An opulent tray ceiling, extraordinary scroll designs in the woodwork, and a wall of Portuguese tile suggest a connoisseur's love of luxury. The cooking area is set behind a counter of smooth green marble, with much of the practical equipment set into the tiled niche, marking this as a kitchen of one who values style as much as function. A settee and dining chairs upholstered in French cotton and voluminous floral drapes complete the extravagant atmosphere.

ABOVE: An interesting ventilation system becomes a piece of floating art in this slick, shiny space. The curving walls and island edges are set off by the angular planes of opposing walls and the geometric stair-step design of the wall cutout. Hard granite, chunky columns, and space-age lighting embody a slinky approach to functional features.

ꕥꕥꕥ

ABOVE: The vast expanse of light oak flooring sets off slate blue walls in a room with a minimalist atmosphere. Though the impression is one of sparseness, there is plenty of cabinetry and shelving to store the pots and pans, serving plates and utensils, cutting boards and bread baskets that seem to reproduce on their own in the kitchen. The curving island houses sinks, stove, and counter space, while the smoked-glass sliding doors on the right-hand wall conceal shelves full of kitchen paraphernalia. A double row of bins on the opposite wall offers additional storage as well as a length of counter that seems downright decadent. Shining stainless steel on refrigerator and over-the-counter cabinets completes the sleek decor.

✻✻✻

ABOVE: Black, white, and a ribbon of honey distinguish this spacious, state-of-the-art kitchen. Set up like a traditional urban galley kitchen, the square footage shown here is liable to make most city dwellers salivate. The warm color of resilient oak flooring couples with tile in an eye-catching pattern reminiscent of quilt blocks to create a feeling of homeyness in an area that might otherwise seem austere.

✹ ✹ ✹

ABOVE: This kitchen is ideal for a cook who likes company—or for one who runs a catering business or gives cooking classes at home. A stretch of hardrock maple atop the island allows helpers to work anywhere that's convenient. The pot rack keeps ladles, baskets, and braids of garlic—as well as the more traditional pots and pans—close at hand. A double oven and side-by-side refrigerators are essential for a family that does a lot of entertaining.

Chapter Six

Elements of an Excellent Kitchen

An excellent kitchen—one that is visually pleasing and delivers an efficient work space—is within reach of all who are willing to take the time to research and design a kitchen for their needs and then follow their plans to completion. Staying focused on problem-solving is important: the main tasks are, first, to find a proper place for everything that goes into the kitchen and, second, to support those design solutions with the proper equipment and furniture.

There are five basic elements that need to be addressed when planning a kitchen: lighting, storage, equipment, surfaces, and furniture. Lighting must be adequate for the tasks at hand and should also create a pleasing ambience in the kitchen. Good storage is essential: without sufficient cabinets, utility drawers, pot racks, and shelving, the cook is forever scrab-

bling about trying to find the right spoon, that big cookie sheet, or the good peppercorns that he or she knows is around someplace. Equipment—the stove, sink, and refrigerator, plus dishwasher and any other appliances—are the heart of the kitchen; from professional ranges to conveniently placed bar sinks, this is a section you'll want to pore over. Whatever the decor of the kitchen, furniture can contribute big design impact as well as serve a truly functional purpose: Welsh dressers, sideboards, and pine tables are hard workers that also provide a graphic link with the past. Finally, beautiful options for surfaces—including walls, floors, and countertops—range from granite worktops to tiled backsplashes to delicately stenciled walls. The pages ahead will bring you scores of possibilities for outfitting every aspect of your kitchen with efficiency and style.

ABOVE: Well-designed, well-made appliances—like this vacuum coffeemaker and stainless steel toaster, both imported from Europe—can last a lifetime. When small appliances are as handsome as these, there's no need to apologize for leaving them on the counter.

❋ ❋ ❋

OPPOSITE: Variety is the name of the game in this kitchen of many surfaces. Whimsical air balloons decorate wall tiles, while the multihued blues of the tiles behind the range top hide spatters until cleanup time. A deliberately unfinished frieze is a rustic counterpoint to the kitchen's polished look. Finally, the island has been treated to a marble top, complete with a dropped-in bar sink.

LIGHTING

Ambient light, supplemented by concentrated task lighting in appropriate places, will result in a room that reflects a serene mood. Note that a bright light placed high on a ceiling can cast unwanted shadows and create harsh edges. Consider bringing the light source down by installing a pendant fixture. Fluorescent lights in newer, more flattering bulb colors and shapes throw soft, natural-looking light that is still highly efficient. Table lamps are a lovely and unusual option, but are only practical if you have a safe place to set them.

Be aware of the disposition of natural light in your room and design your kitchen with that light in mind. If possible, position one of your work areas—a counter, an island, the sink—so that it is flooded with sunlight. This is a natural mood enhancer as well as a practical and energy-efficient source of task lighting. If privacy is not an issue, you may wish to leave windows sans curtains in order to take full advantage of the natural light.

Whatever your lighting choices, remember that lighting is partly a safety issue; you need enough light to see to your kitchen chores without cutting yourself or straining to look at stove settings. Beyond that, the only rule is to find a lighting combination that is flattering to your decor and suits your needs.

ABOVE: Light filtered through a stand of trees imbues molded glass bottles with a gemlike quality. Striped Roman shades can be adjusted to admit or shut out light as the day advances. Tall candlesticks keep flames well away from other table decorations.

OPPOSITE: A grid of ceiling lights provides bright and even illumination in a virtually windowless kitchen. The light-colored cabinets and ceramic floor contribute their considerable reflective power. Traditional outfittings—the wainscoted half-wall, the hanging copper pots, and the simple cabinet design—offset the slightly industrial, futuristic look of the ceiling panels.

ABOVE: A collection of plates and pitchers, lit from below like art objects, introduces a sense of drama in this darkening kitchen. Circular windows add to the theatricality, and shutters at each afford privacy. The shape of the hanging fixture links it clearly to the window, even as its moonlike glow illuminates the island's inlaid cutting board.

✖ ✖ ✖

OPPOSITE: A lengthy stretch of skylights and the pale surface of the floor create a sense of light and space—the feeling is enhanced by the floor-to-ceiling windows and door. Pendant task lighting adds warmth and intimacy to what could otherwise be a chilly atmosphere.

ABOVE: Recessed ceiling lights illuminate the entire kitchen with the help of reflective, soft-hued fawn surfaces and shining stainless steel. Overcounter fluorescent tubes offer the option of additional light close to work spaces.

✲✲✲

ABOVE: Sunshine flooding through tall windows bathes this lovely room in a glow that is both luxurious and cozy. This kitchen area is blessed with a variety of light sources, including twin skylights, hanging globes above the island, recessed task lighting, and a chandelier filled with tapers. This multilayered approach allows you to create the mood and lighting level you want, whether it's soft candlelight for a romantic dinner or a bright spot of light for an intricate project.

ABOVE: Reminiscent of classroom lights, these globes are charming as well as functional. Fluorescent lighting over the counter and stove
coupled with a cylindrical ceiling lamp above the sink supplies sufficient illumination for kitchen chores. When choosing a color for your kitchen, remember that light colors
and white will reflect light, while deep colors will seem to absorb it.

❈❈❈

OPPOSITE: Wide soffits are enclosed with concave panels that conceal and soften the effect of fluorescent bulbs while providing a distinctly modern design element.
Sunshine flowing through the two windows complements the ambient light thrown by the panels.

STORAGE

Taking inventory of the cookware, dishes, table linens, and so on that you do use and editing out the things you don't use are the keys to planning effective storage. After-market storage aids can put your equipment at your fingertips; rollout shelf kits, pot racks, open restaurant shelving, antique cupboards, baskets, hooks, and pegs all offer practical ways to organize the essentials.

If necessary, annex kitchen storage space in other rooms. An armoire in the living room or dining room can house linens, the good china, holiday pieces, and anything else that you don't need every day but want to keep near at hand. Once you have proper storage for all your kitchen things, you'll wonder how you managed in a kitchen where your materials were stored helter-skelter.

ABOVE: A tray drawer provides ample room for stacked quiche dishes, cake pans, and steamer baskets, while multiple slots house trays and baking sheets. Add two deep utility drawers, and this workhorse of an undercounter cabinet becomes every serious cook's dream.

✖ ✖ ✖

OPPOSITE: A glass-fronted jelly cabinet, fitted with a miniature brass knob, shows simple jars and boxes to advantage. The irregular shelves, originally designed to hold different types of jams and preserves, are ideal for storing containers of various shapes and sizes.

✖ ✖ ✖

ABOVE: Open shelves can be practical and quite beautiful if the items are arranged well and kept in pristine condition. The even spacing and vibrant yellow color of these niche shelves give them rhythm and pizzazz.

✳ ✳ ✳

ABOVE: An old, painted cupboard is a treasure trove of tablecloths, napkins, and tea towels, both patterned and plain. China plates and glassware are stored atop the linen cupboard, out of danger of imminent breakage yet still handy enough to use for lazy brunches or afternoon tea. The door of the cabinet, draped with embroidered towels and propped open with a little chair, creates a pleasing still life.

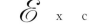

ABOVE LEFT: A pine cupboard with glass doors on top offers plenty of space for a collection of ironstone that deserves display. The roomy cupboard below provides ample storage for those irregular items that are better off left behind closed doors.

ABOVE RIGHT: Flour, grains, dried beans, pastas, and other dry ingredients line the shelves of this efficient little pantry space. Airtight jars are arranged for ease of lifting, with the heaviest placed on bottom shelves. A built-in dresser, made of the same wainscoting as the walls, provides deep drawers for storing table linens and tea towels.

OPPOSITE: Recessed open space is an attractive and practical way to store much-used objects: spices, mixing bowls, and staples are all within arm's length. Note that the textured paint of the walls stops short of the alcove's shelves, avoiding a messy look.

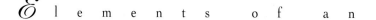

ABOVE LEFT: Pale beech shelving holds a simple but artful arrangement of kitchen paraphernalia. To create an unstudied display, group similar objects of different sizes, such as the identical glass coffeemakers atop the highest shelf. Or, find pieces of different shapes and sizes that share a color, like the creamy white pitchers and teapot. Here, kitchenware in rich brown tones offers pleasing contrasts but preserves a unified look. Don't be afraid to mix kitchen items of varying vintages—theme and color are enough to sucessfully link the pieces

ABOVE RIGHT: Flavored vinegars and oils, put up in tightly corked, molded glass bottles, are a beautiful addition to any kitchen counter. These concoctions capture the essence of summmer; sprinkle them liberally on salads or steamed vegetables, or use them to marinate meat or poultry.

OPPOSITE: The home kitchen of a professional cook relies on a number of restaurant solutions for tricky storage problems. Metro shelving can be assembled in an infinite variety of heights and widths, and can be arranged to suit the layout of the kitchen. Capped with a slab of marble, the top of a low shelf doubles as a baking center. Stacks of Fiestaware and the random tools of the trade, including a flatware caddy straight out of a diner, ornament the open shelves. The overhead pot rack, another fabulous space-saving device, keeps pans and other implements within easy reach.

❉ ❉ ❉

ABOVE: This pantry with adjoining wine cellar is a model of organization. Shallow shelves store easy-to-lose small grocery items; the space saved there has been added to shelving along the opposite wall, which is deep enough to accommodate larger pieces like fruit baskets, paper towels, and cookbooks. Coated wire racks allow wine bottles to be stacked efficiently without danger of rolling.

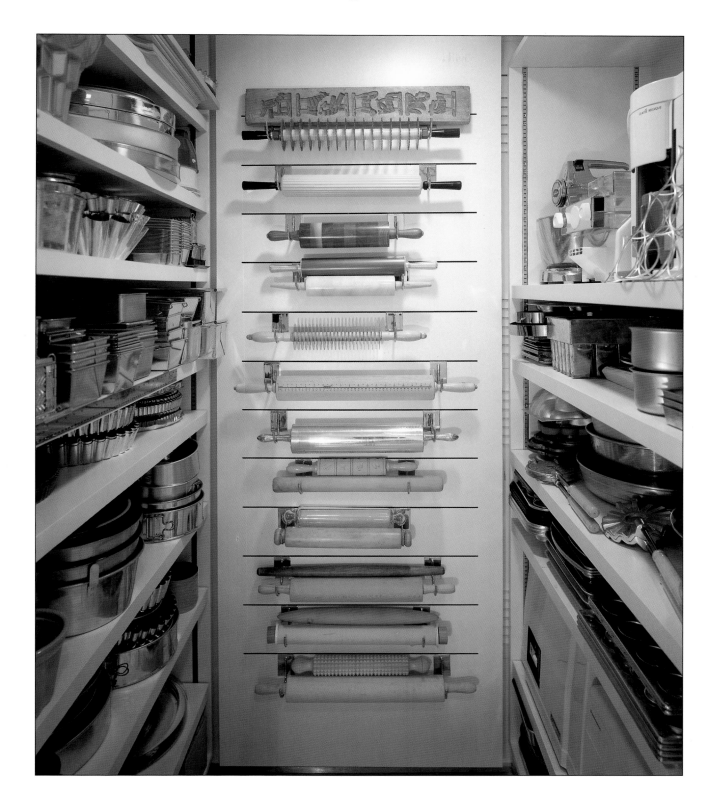

※※※

ABOVE: Adjustable shelves in this baker's closet accommodate random-size equipment without squandering a bit of space. A collection of rolling pins for different purposes and of various vintages is both artful and functional. Storage bins for flour and other dry goods rest easily on low shelves.

ABOVE LEFT: A spice drawer platform holds jars at an angle that makes reading labels easy. While the spice rack is most commonly situated above the stove, a drawer is a better location since spices should ideally be kept in a dark place away from heat.

ABOVE RIGHT: Many new cabinets and drawers are outfitted with wonderfully helpful features. This knife storage drawer is shallow, so as not to waste space, and comes complete with a pullout cutting board. The face of the drawer is outfitted with hinges that allow it to lay flat so that the cutting board can be extended when the drawer in pushed in.

※ ※ ※

ABOVE: An ingenious cutting table rotates out from its permanent home beneath the countertop. This custom-made piece offers a viable solution for cooks seeking a sturdy, easy-access cutting surface. Without the push-back storage feature of this butcher-block slab, only the most extravagant of kitchens could afford to devote space to a counter-size cutting board.

E Q U I P M E N T

Learning about the wonderful equipment now on the market for home kitchens is an adventure in itself. Tour kitchen showrooms, visit home shows, and check out professional restaurant supply showrooms to get an idea of the range of equipment available to you. Remember that your choices for basic equipment are among the most critical decisions you will make in your kitchen.

If you cook for pleasure and enjoy entertaining lavishly, your range choice will be pivotal. Investigate thoroughly the cooking options open to you. Many professionals prefer gas surface burners for the precise control over temperature they afford, while choosing electric ovens that ensure the constant, even heat required for baking and roasting. Make sure to check with your utility company and read local fire and building codes if you plan to introduce any professional equipment into your kitchen. Also, your walls and floors may need special preparation and reinforcing before particularly heavy equipment is brought in.

Rethink refrigeration. Some models allow for separate temperature controls for different parts of the refrigerator; others offer glass doors that render the entire contents visible at a glance; and still others promise amazingly efficient use of space. Undercounter refriger-

ABOVE: Note the pattern of the grids on this gas-fired range top. They meet in a continuous plane, making it easy to slide pans from one burner to another. Be sure to check the BTU output of the burners you plan to install. If you use heavy-duty, professional-quality pans, you will most likely want a ten-thousand- to fifteen-thousand-BTU output from each burner.

OPPOSITE: This triangular brushed steel island has been outfitted with three burners and inlaid with granite to make an exemplary work surface. Matching tables are modular in design, and can be pulled up to the island to provide extra work space or seating for an informal meal, or pushed out of the way to create extra room.

ated drawers put foods where they're most likely to be used. Dairy products and eggs can be stored next to the cooktop; moisture-balanced drawers for caching vegetables can be located right beside the prep sink and chopping surface. These items, once prohibitively expensive, are becoming more competitively priced every year.

The sink setup is another crucial decision: consider installing more than one in order to accommodate all your chores. Deep sinks that can easily hold a stockpot are now widely available, as are smaller sinks designed primarily as water sources. The variety of materials and hardware now available travel far beyond the white porcelain and standard faucets that predominated in the past.

Stove, refrigerator, and sink are the mainstays of the kitchen; if you research well and choose wisely, this homey triumvirate will serve you admirably for years.

ABOVE: A good food processor can take the place of two or three other appliances—including the blender, dough mixer, spice grinder, and mini vegetable chopper—while taking only a third of the space. Because a food processor is so portable, you have a variety of storage options. It can be hidden away in a cabinet or an appliance garage when not in use; it's also compact enough to be left out on the counter, where you're sure to reach for it often.

❋ ❋ ❋

OPPOSITE LEFT: The stainless steel professional refrigerator and freezer are incorporated into a design that makes full use of the shining surface, which is repeated in cabinets and island. The refrigerated drawers at the bottom of each unit, called "fish files" by chefs, are very effective for showing the entire contents at one sweep.

❋ ❋ ❋

OPPOSITE RIGHT: A traditional porcelain, single-bowl sink offers a certain purity and pleasing simplicity. Set onto a synthetic countertop that mimics the look of granite, this size is perfect for small spaces. Note the wrist faucets; designed for hospital use, they enable the user to turn them on and off with just a flick of the wrist (or elbow).

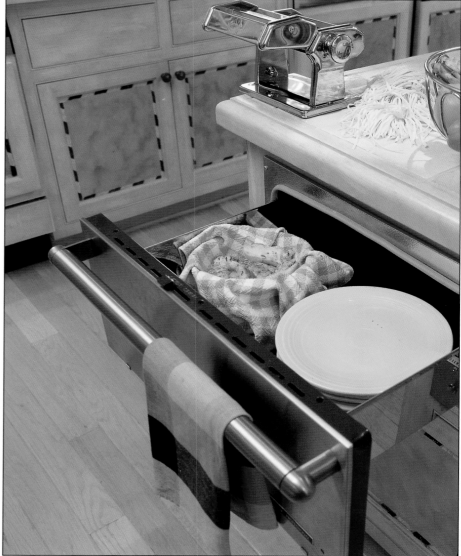

ABOVE LEFT: This fine stove, a sixty-inch (152cm) Garland, is the tried-and-true classic of the restaurant kitchen. It offers six surface burners, a salamander, a griddle, and two ovens. A tiled wall provides the best protection against fire, but you can also install a stainless steel shield for safety's sake.

✺ ✺ ✺

ABOVE RIGHT: The warming drawer, another staple of the professional kitchen, provides low, even heat to keep rolls toasty and to warm a stack of dinner plates. A good warming drawer is an invaluable asset for any cook who likes to entertain, since it relieves the pressure of having to time all the dishes perfectly.

✺ ✺ ✺

OPPOSITE: This professional-style drop-on unit, which combines a charbroiler with a gas range, sits on a tile-topped cabinet. The wavy pattern of the range grids flows over the entire surface, allowing you to set pans anywhere on the unit for either cooking or warming. A pot faucet set into the wall behind the range means you don't have to lug heavy pasta pots full of water from sink to stove.

✖ ✖ ✖

ABOVE: A wall oven can be an excellent alternative to a standard range. Baking and roasting functions can be removed to a part of the kitchen away from the traffic of the more hectic stovetop area. But take care to position wall ovens safely. They should never be placed just beside a doorway: the heat can be transferred to the door jamb and burn those who brush by. Also, make sure that there is room for passage between the open oven door and any counter that faces it. There should also be a heat-resistant surface nearby where you can set hot utensils or roasting pans. Consider installing two ovens if you have a large family or if you like to bake while you prepare other foods.

ABOVE: The professional range has here been given the attention that is its due in the serious cook's kitchen. Its jewellike setting in an emerald-tiled niche is enhanced by squared columns flanking the opening. The hood is covered by a mantle that further emphasizes the importance of the range—a frieze of flowering vines ensures that the piece is supremely decorative. The efficient exhaust system employs filters that are easy to remove and keep clean.

❊ ❊ ❊

ABOVE: A quartz-fired surface drop-in unit requires flat-surfaced pots and pans in order to make contact with the heating element. Controls are unconventionally placed between burners rather than in front of them. A built-in grill offers the luxury of year-round barbecues.

COOKWARE

*P*art of the equipment equation is the decision to acquire new cookware. Any cook will tell you that one of the secrets of success is using quality equipment. The best cookware prevents sticking and distributes heat so that food cooks evenly. Before you buy, consider what you will expect from your pots and pans.

▣ Stainless steel, aluminum, and copper have all been combined in various permutations to bring out the special advantages of each material. Manufacturers are sandwiching these metals together to produce fine equipment with a surface of stainless steel (which is a relatively poor conductor of heat) for easy care, a layer of aluminum to provide good heat distribution, and a bottom coating of copper, which is the best conductor of all.

▣ Anodized aluminum, with its characteristic dark gray sheen, is another popular choice. This material conducts heat beautifully and the finish makes the pans impervious to stains.

▣ Enameled cast iron is a classic. Generations have cooked with this material (sometimes using the very same pot!) and it remains one of the best materials for slow, even cooking. One drawback—it's quite heavy, and thus can be rather unwieldy to handle.

▣ The size and shape of your pans will have considerable impact on your efficiency. If you have purchased newer pans, which are generally larger than old ones, but are still cooking on a thirty-year-old range with small-circumference burners, you won't be able to fit more than three pans on your range. Consider a new range top. Larger pans and burners allow heat to reach food more quickly, accelerating the cooking process. Professional ranges consume more BTUs than smaller units and require heavier, more professional saucepans. It's up to you to balance your cookware needs with the other equipment choices you've made.

▣ Storing the multitude of saucepans and casseroles that a cook inevitably accumulates is not the least of cookware dilemmas. A nineteenth-century-style standing pot rack is the obvious choice. Taking up less than one square foot (0.1 sq m) of space, this decorative and functional tiered rack can stand out of the way in a kitchen corner and hold six or more pots and pans. It's also an easier way to store equipment, since you no longer have to drag heavy pots and lids out of awkward cabinets.

▣ Baking is another kitchen activity that requires specialty equipment. While the shapes of pans and tins are classic, new nonstick materials and air-filled pans make sticking and burning a thing of the past. Make sure that you have the right-size pan for your project, or your bread, brownies, or cake won't have the texture you desire.

▣ Lovely serving pieces bring your creations to the table with style. It isn't necessary to buy a set of expensive matching dishes; a few pieces in traditional shapes and colors will do justice to even the fanciest food.

ABOVE: A clever pullout pan rack, which can be retrofit in an existing cabinet, eliminates the jumble of pans that generally dwells in a low cabinet. This collection sports a pan for every job, from a single omelette to a half dozen burgers.

ABOVE LEFT: Wok cuisine has become increasingly popular, since it is both quick and healthy—two demands that particularly suit today's hectic lifestyle. This special wok stove stands at the ready beneath the countertop—when it's not in use, the entire unit is hidden by a stainless steel cover. In addition to the convenience of having the wok close at hand, the wok stove offers the extremely intense heat that is an important factor in successful wok cooking.

✽✽✽

ABOVE RIGHT: In a period kitchen, modern appliances can sometimes look out of place. Here, the owners have found a creative solution for preserving the atmosphere of their kitchen without sacrificing convenience: the dishwasher is secreted behind a beautifully crafted spice rack. The universal hinge on the door allows it to swing completely out of the way for loading and emptying of the dishwasher.

✽✽✽

OPPOSITE: An elegant European sink makes use of a clay-colored marble with beautiful creamy veins. Marble is a common building material in many countries, and is gaining in popularity worldwide. This deep model is ideal for filling tall vases as well as stockpots. The contrasting marble of the countertop is simply set atop the edges of the marble sink on each side, alleviating the need for the careful caulking that butting slabs would require.

TOP LEFT: Two quarter rounds are an elegant statement at the corner of this gracefully curved counter. The centrally placed tap can fill either sink with ease, while the single mechanism prevents the clutter and awkwardness of placement that the traditional hot and cold faucets would bring.

✳ ✳ ✳

BOTTOM LEFT: A sink for an ambitious cook combines three bowls: reserve one for rinsing fruits, vegetables, and anything else you want to keep soap-free; use another for soaking bowls and dirty utensils as you cook; and leave one free for ongoing cleanup and miscellaneous chores. A retractable faucet head with a spray feature is a good choice for this hardworking unit. Buff-colored tile has been deliberately set unevenly and paint has been purposely aged to contribute a softer look than the gleaming trio of sinks would otherwise allow.

✳ ✳ ✳

ABOVE RIGHT: A charmingly decorated sink is set beneath a counter that incorporates a drain board on one side. This efficient and attractive solution to draining dishes and produce is an old idea that has recently been rediscovered.

❋❋❋

ABOVE: A top-mounted stainless steel sink with two bowls and fitted baskets is perfect for washing delicate vegetables. Top mounting requires a careful fit and professional caulking; unless you're an expert do-it-yourselfer, this is a job best left to a qualified contractor.

FURNITURE

Freestanding furniture in the kitchen is a tried-and-true tradition that was abandoned for a time in past decades, but is enjoying a much-deserved revival. There is nothing like a simple grouping of kitchen table and chairs to represent the warmth and comfort of family life. A good rule to observe when shopping for a kitchen table: buy the biggest one your space will allow. Even if you are single or your family is relatively small, the area will never be wasted as you spread out your projects or welcome friends to a sumptuously set table.

A sideboard and Welsh cupboard are two more pieces that find a welcome home in the kitchen. These charming pieces provide storage and accessibility for dishes and linens while proudly showing off those pieces we choose to display.

Don't be afraid to incorporate nontraditional furniture into your kitchen. A dresser can be filled with table linens, gadgets, and utensils; an upholstered armchair in a corner offers respite from the bustle of the stove area. Allowing yourself to break convention is one of the best parts of taking on the decorating job yourself.

ABOVE: A small, simple cabinet does double duty as a tiny pantry for dry goods and a display area for favorite family collectibles. Four rectangular panes, reminiscent of an outside window, evoke the same cheery feeling.

OPPOSITE: A sturdy pine farm table here replaces the ubiquitous island. The advantage of a table is that it can be moved to the area where you plan to work or can even be set for informal dining. If its legs are fitted with casters, the table is all the more portable. A marble or smooth synthetic surface renders it useful for rolling pastry or setting down piping hot dishes.

ABOVE: Standing just in front of the sink in a stream of sunlight, this antique marble-topped table is poised for work. When considering placement of your preparation area—whether it's a table, a counter, or a bona fide island—make sure that it is situated near water and light sources.

❆ ❆ ❆

OPPOSITE: Texture and warmth are dividends to be had from purchasing well-worn antiques. This vintage pastry worktable lends instant charm to an otherwise unremarkable kitchen. The trough of the table, originally used for mixing dry ingredients and adding liquids, has become a display niche for a delightful collection of egg cups; the raised surface, which once served as the kneading and rolling board, now finds use as a prep area.

❈❈❈

ABOVE: This open living area demands careful attention to the kitchen in order to make the entire room blend seamlessly. Upholstered dining chairs and niche shelving inside the entryway are features that harmonize well with living room furnishings. In turn, the imposing Welsh cupboard is a dignified extension of the tiny kitchen space, and a pine table masquerading as an island has been fitted with a deep vegetable sink. The unsightly plumbing for the sink has been ingeniously hidden by a stocky chest. If you're not handy with tools, a local carpenter can make the necessary adjustments; in this case a hole had to be cut in the top and bottom of the chest to allow the pipes to pass through, and an access panel had to be hewn in the side. This is an attractive and practical solution, but think carefully before you alter a valuable or antique piece—once the saw makes its first mark, there's no turning back.

❈ ❈ ❈

ABOVE: A long dresser (its drawers are on the work side) serves as both a room divider and an island in this comfortable studio space. This arrangement works because of the decorative back of the dresser; many such pieces have unfinished backs, since they were intended to face a wall, so before you adopt this placement, make sure that the back of your dresser is worthy of display. Earthenware jugs filled with utensils decorate the dresser's top, while flatware fills the shallow drawers found at the top of most dressers and table linens occupy the deep lower drawers. A matching dresser against the wall provides additional storage. The armoire is a beautiful and practical solution to the absence of both a proper pantry and sufficient cabinet space.

ABOVE: The traditional farm table, once found at the center of every country home, has reappeared at the heart of the family once again. The scrubbed pine top brooks no worries about marring a pristine surface, and its low height invites little helpers who may not be able to comfortably reach an island. Part of the beauty of a simple table is that it can be matched with any of a number of styles. Here, carved, Mexican-style, rush-seated chairs and a linen cupboard brimming with colorful molas provide a slightly spicy element, though this table would look just as lovely in many other decors, including country, Victorian, or Scandinavian.

OPPOSITE: Corner cupboards have long been lauded as handsome ways to make use of the space that is often lost in angular rooms. This piece is set far enough away from traffic to leave its top doors open, creating an opportunity to display a gorgeous collection of tureens. Lower cabinets may store kitchen equipment, table linens, or a stereo system, an inspired choice for an open kitchen/dining area.

ABOVE: Part of the beauty of antiques is their careworn countenance. Pieces that show their age can assume a place of pride in the kitchen, so don't be too hasty to discard that old cupboard of your grandmother's. Do be sure, however, to pair the piece with other furniture and a setting that are in good condition, or your decor may suffer from an overall impression of shabbiness. This veteran chest does both storage and serving duty against a pristine wall.

❋ ❋ ❋

ABOVE: Rustic furniture and beautifully crafted baskets endow this kitchen with country character. Weighty pieces balance the boxy room—delicate furnishings would tend to be overwhelmed by the stark angles of the built-in cupboard and unadorned walls. Dangling from the pegs of a simple Shaker rack (intended to hold coats and umbrellas) is a collection of finely woven miniature baskets.

ABOVE: A pine sideboard crowned by a plate shelf of another vintage is a startling but effective pairing. The dark knobs of the drawers bind the sideboard visually to the dark wood of the plate shelf. The two pieces offer a wealth of storage and display space for antique china, cookbooks, and even table linens and silver (stashed in the drawers).

✖ ✖ ✖

OPPOSITE: Cobalt and turquoise brighten simple cabinets, imparting a cozy cottage look to this airy kitchen. A sub-zero refrigerator in a matching cobalt is spruced up by white trim, which picks up the porcelain knobs that punctuate drawers and cabinet doors. Color is a natural mood enhancer, and here it offers a cheerful glow and a sense of purity. Note, though, that a low cabinet has been painted a buttery yellow, providing a break for the eye and adding a whisper of serenity to the rather frenetic blues.

ABOVE LEFT: This vintage cupboard takes center stage, celebrating the long life it has seen. Its somewhat primitive construction marks it as a piece that may very well have been homemade. A rubbed, painted surface, worn in all the right places, may be the result of years of overpainting and wear or it may be the product of careful work on a new piece of furniture. While authentic antiques have a glamour all their own, large pieces are often out of the price range of the average buyer. Many furniture dealers now offer reproduction pieces that have been "antiqued" to add the appeal of a well-loved heirloom.

❈ ❈ ❈

ABOVE RIGHT: An old-fashioned worktable, complete with a knife drawer, is paired with an antique butcher block. In the days before kitchen counters, these two surfaces were invaluable for a wide array of kitchen tasks, including cleaning fish, plucking poultry, chopping meat, kneading bread dough, and cutting up fruits and vegetables. Between the wall-hung plate rack and the French pot rack standing beside the butcher block, this corner of the kitchen boasts enough storage space for a complete service for eight with room left over for various casseroles and mixing bowls.

❈ ❈ ❈

OPPOSITE: Even very contemporary settings can benefit from a piece that carries with it the charm of yesteryear. The practicality of the long work space gained speaks for itself, and this sideboard has the added advantage of a lower shelf, which offers extra storage for bowls, pitchers, and other necessities. The logic of investing in a fine piece of furniture like this is flawless: when you move you'll be able to take the piece with you, unlike built-ins and custom-fit cabinets and counters, which must remain behind.

SURFACES

Choosing materials for your surfaces means being aware of all your options, from high-tech materials like stainless steel and Corian to well-loved natural surfaces, such as marble, brick, wood, and stone. Note, though, that most natural materials are extremely porous and must be sealed to prevent staining.

Flooring is a critical part of your new kitchen. A sealed and polished wood floor is resilient and comfortable to walk on, while stone and tile offer color and a strong presence. If you decide on a tile or stone floor, expect to complement it with area rugs in the locations where you stand for long periods of time. Also, stone or tile will feel cold if the room beneath is unheated. A Vinyl tile can be an excellent solution, prized for its variety of colors and the resilience it offers when installed with an underliner. Linoleum, long neglected, has returned with the advent of shapes and colors that can be inlaid, allowing you to design a custom floor rug.

Wall surfaces, too, can do much to enhance your kitchen. From textured looks to bold wallpapers to trompe l'oeil treatments, there are scores of fabulous options. And don't forget backsplashes—these areas above stove or sink serve a practical purpose, but can be highly decorative as well.

Consider the style of your kitchen, the type of wear the surface is likely to encounter, and the amount you plan to spend, then make your surface choices accordingly. With just a little research, you can be assured of beautiful, practical surfaces for years to come.

ABOVE: Shards of tile in brilliant hues and patterns reminiscent of twentieth-century stained glass design prove highly ornamental on this sink surround. The randomly shaped pieces are accented by the occasional flower, heart, or star, offering a representational reprieve in a sea of abstraction.

OPPOSITE: A Japanese-style still life on painted tile is simple yet evocative in this elegant, light-filled kitchen. The decorative tile frame for the "painting" is repeated as a border for the countertop, providing a sense of unity, which is subtly reinforced by the rhythmic corner design of the wall tiles. With the abundance of painted tile in evidence, the functional Corian counter needs no embellishment.

ABOVE LEFT: Multicolored mosaic tiles make up a Klimtlike pattern on this backsplash and counter. As practical as it is decorative, this arrangement—with its rainbow of colors—won't show spatters or spills. And the smooth curve of wall to horizontal surface means no tough-to-reach corners to clean. The vast number of colors used opens a range of possibilities for cabinet and floor choices.

✳ ✳ ✳

ABOVE RIGHT: The ancient border pattern of rolling waves washes across this stylish backsplash. An inner border of teal "bricks" offers a much-needed transition between the outer border and the harlequin pattern of the field. Tile—which we love for the color and reflected light it contributes—is also the best insulator for the wall behind a grill.

✳ ✳ ✳

OPPOSITE: Even the hood has been treated to tiles painted with birds, bows, and blossoms in this highly decorated kitchen. Bullnose tiles bordering the island top, as well as select tiles across the surface, are likewise in a perpetual ode to spring. Cabinet surfaces have been pickled for a light effect and, in an unusual move, the ceiling has been papered to resemble latticework. The lovely, bowerlike decor is one generally reserved for bedrooms and bathrooms, but with a little creativity has been adapted to the functional quality of the kitchen.

ABOVE: Teak cabinetry and granite counters create an oriental simplicity in this room with a view. Sparse decoration allows the beauty of the surfaces to take center stage. As in many Japanese-inspired rooms, nature provides both the theme for the kitchen and a focal point beyond it.

✳ ✳ ✳

OPPOSITE: Granite offers everything you'd look for in a countertop—beauty, durability, and ease of care. Unfortunately, it is both expensive and heavy, often requiring special handling and installation. Before you order granite surfaces, be sure that your cabinetry can support the weight of the slab. If it can't, don't lose hope: you may be able to have a carpenter reinforce the structure to hold the granite's weight.

ABOVE LEFT: A small but stunning kitchen replete with polished wood surfaces hints at the upscale urban kitchens of the late nineteenth century. The parquet floor has been inlaid with diamond-shaped marble tiles, creating a "pathway" through the kitchen to the dining area. White marble countertops lighten the effect of dark wood while remaining consistent with the formality of the theme.

❊ ❊ ❊

ABOVE RIGHT: A selection of quotations stenciled above soffits makes a decorative and truly refined frieze. The aging process of the new wall has been helped along a bit with an artist's brush (note the re-created water stains and plaster imperfections), matching the careworn air of stately wooden cabinets. "Antiquing" surfaces of structures and furniture has become a popular way to combine the usefulness of new objects with the charm of vintage pieces.

❊ ❊ ❊

OPPOSITE: An unusual floral in a deep blue covers walls, ceiling, and upper cabinets in this long galley kitchen. The use of a single pattern both unifies and enlarges the narrow space; a subtle strip in the Roman shades is a welcome counterpoint to the wash of blooms. Maple countertops and a parquet floor in a classic herringbone pattern, together with the bold use of pattern, add drama and style to a small city kitchen.

ABOVE LEFT: Matching your surface choices to your decor is a good way to achieve continuity and allows you to take a more eclectic approach with furniture and accessories without sacrificing the impact of your theme. Stucco walls are perfectly in keeping with the Southwest theme of this airy kitchen, as are the exposed planks and beams of the ceiling, which are typical of adobe construction. Chairs with rush seats and backs are reminiscent of the folk chairs of Mexico and a Spanish *santos* figure stands on a small shelf above a row of utensils, further evoking the traditions of the American Southwest.

❈ ❈ ❈

ABOVE RIGHT: Stone paired with wood lends a sense of timelessness to this understated space. Square-cut flagstone tiles grace a stub wall that surrounds the sink and range top, effectively blocking the work surface from view. The smooth, subtly mottled character of the tiles echoes the unadorned but beautifully grained wood cabinetry, while the use of mixed woods prevents the expansive surfaces from appearing monotonous.

❈ ❈ ❈

OPPOSITE: Wide-plank flooring and cabinetry in knotty pine unify this country kitchen and ground it in a romantic past despite the new materials used for countertops and appliances. The Formica of the counters is a matte blue-black, de-emphasizing a synthetic quality and mimicking the look of natural slate. Note that the Formica countertops have rounded corners, which soften that material, complementing the worn edges of the unfinished wooden beams that punctuate the ceiling, walls, and doorways. Shaker pieces such as the plate rack, wall sconce, and tape-back chairs add to the overall simplicity of the room.

FURTHER READING

Allen, Sam. *Making Kitchen Cabinet Accessories.* New York: Sterling, 1990.

Beckstrom, Robert J. *Designing and Remodeling Kitchens.* Rev. ed. San Ramon, Calif.: Ortho Books, 1990.

Better Homes and Gardens editors. *Better Homes and Gardens Step-by-Step Cabinets and Shelves.* Des Moines: Meredith Books, 1983.

Bollinger, Don. *Hardwood Floors: Laying, Sanding, and Finishing.* Newtown, Conn.: Taunton, 1990.

Branson, Gary D. *The Complete Guide to Floors, Walls, and Ceilings: A Comprehensive Do-It-Yourself Handbook.* Betterway Books, 1992.

Bridge, Fred, and Jean F. Tibbetts. *The Well-Tooled Kitchen.* New York: Morrow, 1992.

Brumbaugh, James E. *Wood Furniture: Finishing, Refinishing, Repairing.* 3rd ed. New York: Macmillan, 1992.

Byrne, Michael. *Setting Ceramic Tile.* Newtown, Conn.:Taunton, 1987.

Carey, Jere. *Building Your Own Kitchen Cabinets.* Newtown, Conn.: Taunton, 1983.

Conran, Terence. *Terence Conran's Kitchen Book.* New York: Overlook Press, 1993.

Emmerling, Mary. *Mary Emmerling's American Country South.* New York: Clarkson Potter, 1989.

Giorgini, Frank. *Handmade Tiles: Designing, Making, Decorating.* Asheville, N.C.: Lark Books, 1994.

Goldbeck, David. *The Smart Kitchen.* 2nd ed. Ceres Press, 1994.

Grosslight, Jane. *Lighting Kitchens and Baths*, How-to-Book Interior Design series. Durwood, 1993.

Grotz, George. *The Furniture Doctor: A Guide to the Care, Repair, and Refinishing of Furniture.* New York: Doubleday, 1989.

Hillard, Elizabeth. *Designing with Tiles.* New York: Abbeville Press, 1993.

House Beautiful magazine editors. *House Beautiful Kitchens.* New York: Hearst Books, 1993.

How to Re-Do Your Kitchen Cabinets and Counter Tops, Home Care Guides series. New York: Simon & Schuster, 1981.

Hughes, Brad. *The Complete Guide to Restoring and Maintaining Wood Furniture and Cabinets.* Betterway Books, 1993.

Hutton. *Kitchen and Bath Source Book.* New York: McGraw-Hill, 1993.

Innes, Jocasta. *The New Paint Magic.* New York: Pantheon, 1992.

Jones, Charyn. *The Painted Kitchen: Ideas and Inspiration for the Creative Home Decorator.* New York: Sterling, 1994.

Krasner, Deborah. *Planning the Perfect Kitchen: Professional Solutions for Home Cooks.* New York: Studio Books, 1994.

Lindberger, Jan. *The Fifties and Sixties Kitchen: A Handbook and Price Guide.* Atglen, Penn.: Schiffer, 1994.

Litchfield, Michael. *Decorating with Architectural Details*, For Your Home series. New York: Friedman/Fairfax, 1995.

Manroe, Candace. *Floor Treatments*, For Your Home series. New York: Little, Brown, 1994.

——. *Lighting Ideas*, For Your Home series. New York: Little, Brown, 1994.

Miller, Judith. *Period Kitchens: A Practical Guide to Period-Style Decorating.* Wappingers Falls, N.Y.: Antique Collectibles Club Ltd., 1995.

Mircovich, Rhonda. *Palatable Pantries and Lavish Larders.* Distinctive, 1993.

Plant, Tim. *Painted Illusions: A Creative Guide to Painting Murals and Trompe L'oeil Effects.* New York: Sterling, 1991.

Rees, Yvonne, and Tony Herbert. *Floor Style: A Sourcebook of Ideas for Transforming the World Beneath Your Feet.* New York: Chapman and Hall, 1989.

Sayer-Faye, Rebecca. *Country Living New Country Kitchens.* New York: Hearst Books, 1995.

Sloan, Annie, and Kate Gwynne. *Classic Paints and Faux Finishes: How to Use Natural Materials and Authentic Techniques in Today's Decorating.* Pleasantville, N.Y.: Reader's Digest, 1993.

Time-Life Books editors. *Kitchens: Home Repair and Improvement.* New York: Time-Life, 1994.

SOFTWARE

3-D Kitchen. Palo Alto, Calif.: Books That Work.

SOURCES

United States

Advice

American Institute of Architects
1735 New York Avenue NW
Washington, DC 20006
202-626-7300

American Society of Interior Designers
608 Massachusetts Avenue NE
Washington, DC 20002
202-546-3480

Gas Appliance Manufacturers Association
1901 North Moore Street
Suite 1100
Arlington, VA 22209
703-525-9565

Granite Industries of Vermont
Barre, VT 05641
802-479-2202

Hardwood Manufacturers Association
400 Penn Center Boulevard
Suite 530
Pittsburgh, PA 15235
412-829-0770

National Association of Plumbing,
Heating, and Cooling Contractors
P.O. Box 6808
Fall Church, VA 22040
703-237-8100

National Kitchen and Bath Association
687 Willow Grove Street
Hackettstown, NJ 07840-9988
908-852-0033

Ranges and Cookers

AGA
RFD 1, Box 477
Stowe, VT 05672
802-253-9727

Dacor
950 South Raymond Avenue
Pasadena, CA
818-305-7616

Five-Star
Brown Stove Works
P.O. Box 2490
Cleveland, TN 37320
800-251-7485

Garland
Garland Commercial Industries
185 East South Street
Freeland, PA 18224
717-636-1000

General Electric
GE Appliances
Appliance Park
Louisville, KY 40225
800-626-2000

Russel Range
325 South Maple Avenue, #5
South San Francisco, CA 94080
415-873-0105

Thermador
5119 District Boulevard
P.O. Box 22129
Los Angeles, CA 90022
800-656-9226

Twikivi
The New Alberne Stove Co.
P.O. Box 300
Schuyler, VA 22969
804-831-2228

Viking
Viking Range Corp.
111 Front Street
P.O. Drawer 956
Greenwood, MS 38930
601-455-1200

Vulcan
Food Service Equipment
P.O. Box 696
Louisville, KY 40201
502-778-2791

Wolf
Wolf Range Co.
19600 South Alameda Street
Compton, CA 90221
310-637-3737

Refrigerators

Amana Refrigeration
Amana, IA 52204
800-843-0304

Frigidaire
6000 Perimeter Drive
Dublin, OH 43017
800-365-1365

General Electric
GE Appliances
Appliance Park
Louisville, KY 40225
800 626-2000

Sub-Zero
P.O. Box 44130
Madison, WI 53744-4130
608-271-2233

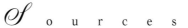

Traulsen
114-02 15th Avenue
College Point, NY 11356
718-463-9000

Cabinetry and Fittings

Elfa
300-3A Route 17 South
Lodi, NJ 07644
201-777-1554

Ikea
Ikea USA Headquarters
Plymouth Meeting Mall
Plymouth Meeting, PA 19462
610-834-0150

KraftMaid Cabinetry
P.O. Box 1055
16052 Industrial Parkway
Middlefield, OH 44062
216-632-5333

Specialty Woodworking
166 Water Street
Brooklyn, NY 11201
718-403-0456

Timberlake Cabinet Co.
3102 Shawnee Drive
P.O. Box 1990
Winchester, VA 22601
800 388-2483

Wood-Mode, Inc.
1 Second Street
Kreamer, PA 17833
717-374-2711

Surfaces

American Olean Tile Co.
100 Cannon Avenue
Lansdale, PA 19446
215-855-1111

Armstrong World Industries
P.O. Box 3001
Lancaster, PA 17604
800 233-3823

Bruce Hardwood Floors
16803 Dallas Parkway
Dallas, TX 75248
800 722-4647

Busby-Gilbert Tile Co.
16021 Arminta Street
Van Nuys, CA 91406
818-780-9460

Color Tile
515 Houston Street
Fort Worth, TX 76102
817-870-9538

Corian Products
DuPont Co.
PPD Dept
Wilmington, DE 19898
800 4-CORIAN

Formica Corporation
10155 Reading Road
Cincinnati, OH 45241
513-786-3533

Hastings Tile
30 Commercial Street
Freeport, NY 11520
516-379-3500

Italian Tile Center
Division of the Italian Trade Commission
499 Park Avenue
New York, NY 10022
212-980-1500

Mannington Resilient Floors
P.O. Box 30
Salem, NJ 08079
609-935-3000

Vermont Marble Co.
61 Main Street
Proctor, VT 05765
800-451-4468

Sinks and Hardware

American Standard, Inc.
1 Centennial Plaza
P.O. Box 6820
Piscataway, NY 08855-6820
201-980-3000

Kohler Co.
Kohler, WI 53044
414-457-1271

Water Faucets
3001 Redhill
Building 5, Suite 108/145
Costa Mesa, CA 92626
800-243-4H2O

Lighting

George Kovacs Lighting, Inc.
67-25 Otto Road
Glendale, NY 11385
718-392-8190

Halo Lighting
6 West 20th Street
New York, NY 10011
212-645-4580

Lightolier Inc.
100 Lighting Way
Secaucus, NJ
201-864-3000

Furniture, Housewares, and Cookware

ABC Carpet and Home
888 Broadway
New York, NY 10003
212-473-3000

All-Clad
All-Clad Metal Crafters, Inc.
RD 2
Cannonsburg, PA 15317
412-745-8300

Calphalon Commercial Aluminum
    Cookware Co.
Department 55
P.O. Box 583
Toledo, OH 43693

Commercial Culinary
P.O. Box 30010
Alexandria, VA 22310
800 999-4949

Crate & Barrel
725 Landwehr Road
Northbrook, IL 60062
708-272-2888

Ikea
Ikea USA Headquarters
Plymouth Meeting Mall
Plymouth Meeting, PA 19462
610-834-0150

Pottery Barn
P.O. Box 7044
San Francisco, CA 94120-7044
800 927-5507

Williams-Sonoma
P.O. Box 7456
San Francisco, CA 94120
800 541-2233

Miscellaneous

Gardener's Eden
P.O. Box 7307
San Francisco, CA 94120-7307
800 541-2233

Gardener's Supply Catalogue
128 Intervale Road
Burlington, VT 05401
802-863-1700

Hard-to-Find Tools Catalogue
5 Vose Farm Road
P.O. Box 803
Peterborough, NH 03460-0803
603-924-9541

Hold Everything
P.O. Box 7807
San Francisco, CA 94120-7807
800 541-2233

The Home Depot
2727 Paces Ferry Road
Atlanta, GA 30339
404-433-8211

Canada

Anderson Kitchen Design
70 Colonnade Road
Nepean, Ontario K2E 702
613-225-9555

Carter's Kitchen Centre
Richmond Street North
Arva (London), Ontario N0M IC0
519-660-8445

Contour Kitchen Design
1128 Mainland Road
Vancouver, British Columbia V6B 5L1
604-682-0545

Countrywide Kitchens
407 Counter Street, #110
Kingston, Ontario K7K 6A9
613-549-8650

Hanover Kitchens
79 Shepherd's Avenue West
Toronto, Ontario M2N 1M4
416-512-7979

Jake Klassen's Kitchen Gallery
430-432 Kensington
Winnipeg, Manitoba R3J 1J7
204-989-6400

The Kitchen Emporium
54 Kent Street
Woodstock, Ontario N4S 6Y7
519-537-7180

The Kitchen Place
861 Simco Street South
Oshawa, Ontario L1H 4K8
905-579-2417

Merit Kitchen Centre
2401 Burrard Street
Vancouver, British Columbia V6J 3J3
604-736-2966

Oakville Kitchen Centre
599 Third Line
Oakville, Ontario L6L 4A8
905-827-4611

Town & Country Kitchens
17212 107th Avenue
Edmonton, Alberta T5S 1E9
403-489-3331

PHOTOGRAPHY CREDITS

©William Abranowicz: pp. 29, 65, 129 left, 134

Courtesy of Aristokraft, Inc.: p. 132 right

©BOFFI/Esprit: Design: Piero Lissoni: pp. 67, 109

©BOFFI/Grand Chef: Design: Tanzi: p. 69

©Kelly Bugden: pp. 85, 124, 138 left

©Grey Crawford: pp. 47, 131; Architecture: Lawerce Allen: p. 116; Architecture: Steven Erhlich: p. 46; Architecture: Lisa Matthews: p. 35

©Derrick & Love: Design: Derrick & Love: p. 59 left; Design: Grandberg Architects: p. 120; Design: Stephen Mallory: p. 118

©Daniel Eifert: Design: Bogdanow & Asociates: p. 76; Design: David Whitcomb: p. 60

©Philip Ennis: Design & Architecture: Audio/Video/Interiors & M.J. Macaluso & Associates: p. 59 right; Design: Pierre Deux by Motif Designs: pp. 28 right, 62; Design: Beverly Ellsley: p. 53; Design: Four Seasons Green Houses: p. 66; Design: Gail Green: pp. 112, 136; Design: Ken Hockin Interior Decoration: p. 161; Architecture: Mojo Stumer Architects: p. 28 left; Design: Motif Designs: pp. 57, 126 left; Design: Barbara Ostrom: pp. 51, 107; Design: Tom O'Tool: p. 169 left; Design: Vogel/Mulea Designs: pp. 71, 72, 147

Courtesy of/Design by: P.J. Falco & Associates: pp. 2–3

©Feliciano: pp. 15, 30 left, 37, 90

©Michael Garland: Design: Peggy Butcher: p. 27 left; Architecture: Fred Fishor: p. 12; Design: Sunday Hendrickson: p. 14; Design: Judy Kenyon: p. 40; Design: Kelsey Maddox-Bell: pp. 100, 127; Architecture: Parkinson Field Associates: pp. 44, 114; Design: Joe Ruggeiro: pp. 144 right, 152; Design: Peter Shire: p. 45

©Tria Giovan: pp. 133, 143; Design: Ken Fishman: p. 74 left; Design: Michael Foster: p. 155; Design: Charles Riley: pp. 10, 82; Design: Anna Thomas: pp. 87, 153

©David Henderson: p. 123

©Nancy Hill: p. 148; Courtesy of House Beautiful's Kitchen & Bath Magazine: p. 106 right; Courtesy of House Beautiful's Home Remodeling & Decorating Magazine: pp. 31, 151; Architecture: Robert Davis: p. 132 left; Design: Kitchens by Deane, CT: pp. 61, 73, 98; Design: Mary Fisher Design, RSPI: p. 16; Design: Hammer & Nail, Inc.: p. 56; Design: Robert Nevins: p. 103; Design: Siegel Design Group: p. 121

©image/dennis krukowski: p. 78 (from: The Farmhouse, Bentam); Design: Tonin Mac Callum ASID, Inc.: pp. 84, 168; Design: Robert Metzger Interiors, Inc./Michael Christiano Assoc.: p. 83; Design: Gary Jay Paul Architecture & Decorating: pp. 80, 81

Courtesy of Jennaire: p. 142

©John Kane: pp. 104, 125, 158

Courtesy of Kohler Co.: p. 146 all

©Balthazar Korab: pp. 43, 89, 170 left

©Brian Leatart: pp. 70, 94 left, 102, 111, 129 right, 139, 160 right, 165

©Tim Lee: pp. 91, 106 left; Design: Cold Spring Design: p. 99; Design: Putnam Kitchens: p. 39

©Jennifer Levy: Architecture: Bartos & Rhodes: p. 117; Cabinetry and Millwork: Philip Matsu, Specialty Construction, Brooklyn, New York: p. 22 both; Design: Mojo-Stumer: pp. 58, 108

©David Livingston: pp. 11, 21, 23, 26, 30 right, 34, 36 left, 41, 77 left, 86, 92, 97, 141, 154, 157, 164 right, 166, 167, 169 right

©Mark Lohman: Design: Judith Kanner: p. 75; Design: Janet Lohman: p. 13; Design: Cynthia Marks: pp. 138 right, 156

©Richard Mandlekorn: p. 137; Design: The Cooper Group: p. 110; Design: Stedila Design: p. 170 right

©Robert Perron: Architecture: Paul Bailey: p. 54; Architecture: Charles Sieger: p. 50, Design: Solsearch: p. 64; Design: Rick Wineshenk: p. 93

©David Phelps: Courtesy of American Homestyle & Gardening Magazine: pp. 17, 33; Design: Linda Chase, Carlson Chase Associates, New York and Los Angeles: pp. 38, 164 left; Courtesy of First for Women Magazine: p. 162; Design: Alicia Orrick, Greenwich, CT: p. 79; Design: Florence Perchuk, New York, Courtesy of Food & Wine Magazine: p. 105; Design & Architecture: Kevin Walz, New York, Courtesy of American Homestyle & Gardening Magazine: p. 25; Courtesy of Food & Wine Magazine: p. 126 right

©Eric Roth: p. 122; Design: Crown Point Cabinetry, Clairemont, NH: p. 55; Architecture: Olson Lewis Architects, Manchester, MA: p. 96; Architecture: Robert Miklos, principal, Schwartz Silver Architects, Boston, MA: p. 128

©Bill Rothschild: pp. 18, 94 right, 113, 119, 140

©Richard Sexton: p. 130

©Tim Street-Porter: p. 63; Design: Archer: p. 27 right; Design: Bob and Isabel Higgins: p. 159; Design: Annie Kelly: p. 160 left; Design: Mark Mack: p. 48; Design: Brian Murphy: pp. 42, 135; Design: Larry Totah: p. 68, Design: Wilkinson: p. 88; Design: Mark Rios: p. 145

©Jessie Walker: Design: Donna Aylesworth, ASID, Stkins & Aylesworth, Hinsdale, IL: p. 163; Architecture: Ken Behles, Behles & Behles, Evanston, IL: p. 150; Design & Architecture: Linda Grubb, Barrington, IL: p. 74 right; Architecture: David Hirschman, Chicago, IL: p. 20; Design: Jeffrey Lawrence, ISID, Lawrence Interiors, Lake Bluff, IL: p. 32; Design: David McFadden, Geneva, IL: p. 19; Lani Myron, Susan Fredman Associates, Chicago, IL: p. 101; Design: Janie Petkus, ISID, Hinsdale, IL: p. 36 right; Design: Arlene Semel, ASID, Arlene Semel Associates, Chicago, IL: p. 149; Design: Susan Simonetti: p. 24; Architecture: Claudia Skylar, Mastro Skylar Associates, Chicago, IL: p. 52; Jessie Walker Associates: p. 115; Design: Lee Youngstrom & Susan Reese, Interiors II, Barrington, IL: p. 77 right

©Paul Warchol: pp. 49, 136 right

INDEX

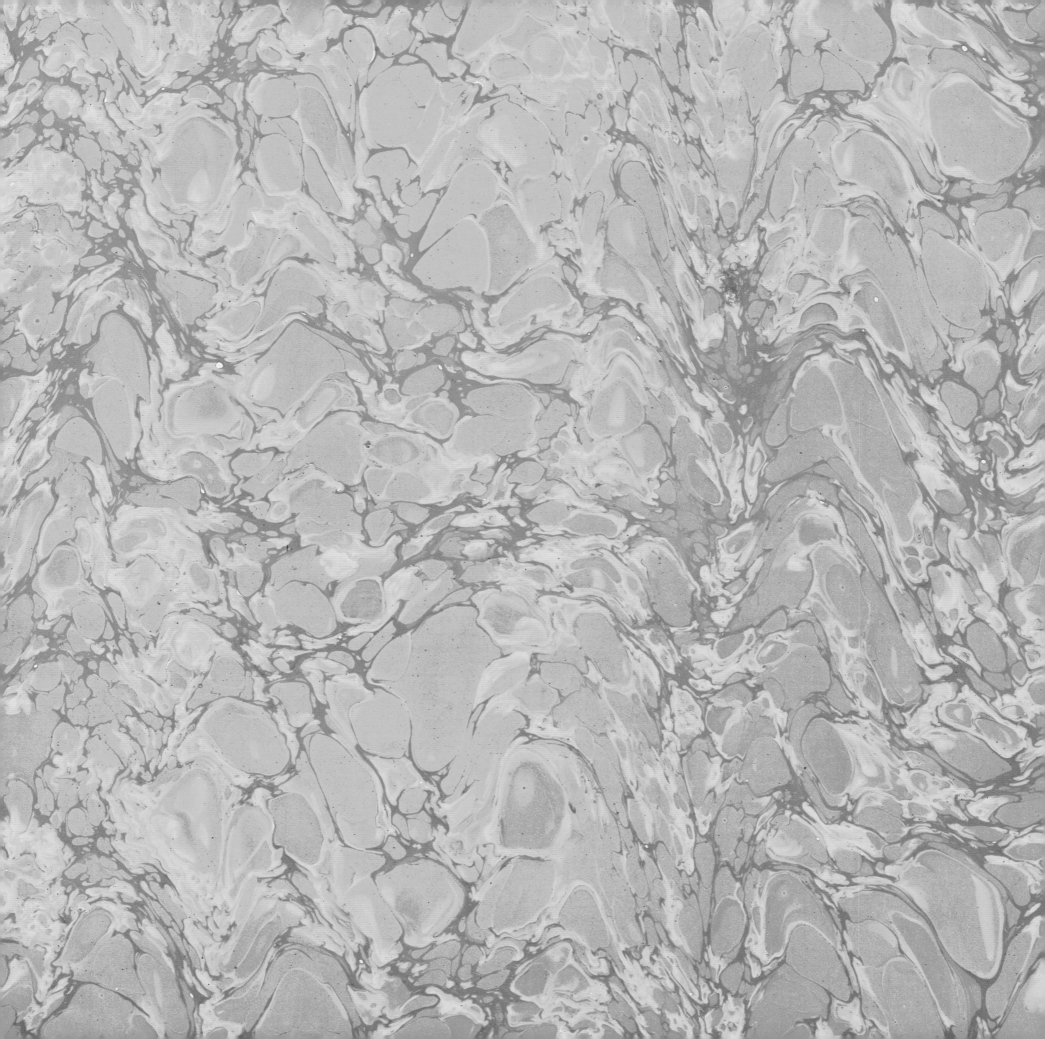